YOUR
SURRENDER

JESUS, YOU AND THE CROSS

DR. CELESTE OWENS

GOOD SUCCESS PUBLISHING

The Art of Your Surrender
©2016 by Dr. Celeste Owens

This book is also available as an ebook.
Visit www.drcelesteowens.com

All rights reserved. No part of this publication may be reproduced, stored in a retrieval system, or transmitted in any form or by any means—electronic, mechanical, photocopy, recording, or any other—except for brief quotations in printed reviews, without the prior permission of the publisher.

Requests for information should be addressed to:

> Good Success Publishing,
> P.O. Box 5072, Upper Marlboro, MD 20775

ISBN 978-0-9837895-2-9

Library of Congress Control Number: 2016908300

This book is printed on acid-free paper

All scripture quotations, unless otherwise indicated, are taken from the New King James Version. Used by permission. All rights reserved.

Cover design: August Pride, LLC
Interior design: Electronic Quill Publishing Services

Printed in the United States of America

Dedicated to AJ and Aaliyah.
May you know the power of surrender.

Table of Contents

Foreword

Can I be honest? I used to wish Matthew 16:24 wasn't in the Bible. I was fine with Psalm 23 and all God's promises to bless me. But this verse made me extremely uncomfortable. Here's why: My heart, like yours, longs for joy and fulfillment. How was I going to taste joy and fulfillment following these heart-penetrating words of Jesus? *"If any man wishes to come after me, let him deny himself, take up his cross and follow me."*

Surrender is a total act of faith because it means giving up control. Control is rooted in fear; surrender is rooted in love.

Here's the bottom line. God is the perfect gentlemen. He will never force His will on us. But apart from surrendering to Him life is filled with futility, fruitlessness and frustration.

In her timely book, *The Art of Your Surrender: Jesus, You and the Cross* my friend Dr. Celeste Owens helps us know it is only through "surrender" we discover our true life, ultimate purpose and unspeakable joy.

The process simply laid out in *The Art of Your Surrender* will . . .

- Deepen your love for Jesus
- Expose idols such as fear, striving and control
- Transform your heart from restlessness to rest
- Help you discover real significance and identity as God's son/daughter

You really want to live your best life? Surrender your current life today and every day.

The Art of Your Surrender: Jesus, You and the Cross will show you the way.

Dr. Johnny Parker
Director of Spiritual Cares and Men's Ministry,
First Baptist Church Glenarden
Former Chaplain of Washington Redskins

Introduction

There is an art to surrendering and I have written this book to simplify its process. That's not to imply that there is anything simple about surrendering; indeed, it takes the supernatural power of the Father to get it right; however, when one surrenders completely, it makes life simple.

I know this first-hand. At the end of 2008, at what I thought was the height of my career God instructed me to leave it all. For what, I wasn't sure, but in obedience to God I did just that.

By the end of 2009, I had left a flourishing private practice, a national speaking platform, writing commitments to several prominent online magazines and newspapers, and my role as ministry leader at my church. And at the top of 2010 I found myself at home waiting on my next steps. The wait wasn't easy. In fact, the wait was painful, but it was necessary.

There is a scripture in the Bible that sums up surrendering as this, "If anyone desires to come after Me, let him deny himself, and take up his cross, and follow Me" (Matthew 16:24).

The scripture speaks volumes for where I was in 2010. I desired with everything that was in me to come after Jesus. In fact, my compliance with the Godly directive to *deny myself, pick up my cross and follow Him* was what catapulted me to my next greater position in the kingdom.

How much do you desire Jesus? Are you willing to leave it all?

Surrendering is not to be feared; it doesn't imply defeat. In fact, in God's economy surrender equals freedom and victory. When you surrender to God, you are not a victim but a willing partner in a plan that will change the world and advance His kingdom.

I know this for sure, at some point in your life God will bring you to a place of surrender. My prayer is that you answer that call with a "Yes".

Jesus Predicts His Death and Resurrection
(Matthew 16:21–26)

[21] From that time Jesus began to show to His disciples that He must go to Jerusalem, and suffer many things from the elders and chief priests and scribes, and be killed, and be raised the third day.

[22] Then Peter took Him aside and began to rebuke Him, saying, "Far be it from You, Lord; this shall not happen to You!"

[23] But He turned and said to Peter, "Get behind Me, Satan! You are an offense to Me, for you are not mindful of the things of God, but the things of men."

[24] Then Jesus said to His disciples, "If anyone desires to come after Me, let him deny himself, and take up his cross, and follow Me.

²⁵ For whoever desires to save his life will lose it, but whoever loses his life for My sake will find it.

²⁶ For what profit is it to a man if he gains the whole world, and loses his own soul? Or what will a man give in exchange for his soul?

ONE

Surrender Keeps Me Focused

"You are not mindful of the things of God,
but the things of men."

What would your life look like if you were truly mindful of the things of God? If you were operating in His strength and not your own? If you were fully surrendered to His agenda, His plans, His wants? Would your life look like what it looks like now, or would some changes be in order?

Being mindful of the things of God takes a full surrender of the heart, mind, will, and emotions. It requires you to do God's will, His way and to yield

1

what you want and put Him at the center. When God is allowed to be the center, we talk, walk, think, and live as such. Our conversations are God-directed, our interactions are pleasing to Him, and our pursuit of dreams, ambitions, and goals are done so with a reverence for His will and plan.

So often in life, with all of its ups and downs and opportunities for distraction, we become more mindful of the things of men than of God; we merely see things from a human point of view, not from God's. The human point of view is shallow. It seeks to live a life that brings only comfort, ease, and simplicity. Many misguided Christians accept Jesus as their Lord and Savior with the belief that they just bought a ticket to easy street. However, the phrase *pick up your cross and follow me* implies the contrary. Life with Jesus is a life of peace and joy, not because there are no problems, but because He is the problem-solver and His strength is made perfect in our weakness.

In Matthew 16:22–23, we are witness to an interaction between Jesus and Peter that demonstrates precisely the points made above. Jesus was surrendered and mindful of the things of God, while well-meaning Peter was guided by and mindful of the things of men.

In Peter's defense, Jesus had just dropped a bombshell on him and the others. *He would die a criminal's death?* That wasn't the plan they had for Jesus. The Messiah they had conjured in their minds was a strong and glorious earthly king whose purpose was to deliver them from their Roman oppressors and form, once again, a great and independent Jewish kingdom. So Jesus' prediction of His death left them bewildered and confused. So I'm guessing the others elected Peter to talk some sense into Jesus; He needed to know that they would follow Him to the ends of the earth, as long as He led where they expected Him to go.

Before you go judging the disciples, how often do you box God into the image of who you think He should be? How often have you boxed Him into a plan that you considered foolproof only to discover that He had an entirely different plan in mind; a plan you were sure would fail or worse, cause you pain? Perhaps that was a little of what Peter and the others felt as they listened to their Lord and Savior predict His death. To their dismay, Jesus wasn't focused on and mindful of His comfort or theirs, but mindful of the things of God. He was convinced that God's bigger dream was worth living.

Let's be clear—God can dream a bigger dream than you. No matter what you are going through right now, God's plans for your life have not changed. As stated in Jeremiah 29:11, His thoughts and plans of peace and not evil for you are still true. As the disciples came to learn, His dream for them was far greater than deliverance from the government of that day. His bigger dream was that they would take the world by storm with the message of the Gospel. That they would open blinded eyes, cause the lame to walk, cast out demons and deliver a message of hope and deliverance well beyond their territory. But that could only happen when they became mindful of the things of God.

IT'S NOT ABOUT YOU

As a babe in Christ—not implying that I was newly converted, but rather that I possessed a mindset that lacked maturity in the ways of Christ—I summed up the Christian life as such: *when I do good I am rewarded and when I do bad I am punished.* That destructive thought pattern caused me to be entangled in a "works" gospel that had less to do with cultivating an authentic relationship with God, and more to do with pretending to be all good all the time so I could get more and more of what I wanted from God.

So imagine my distress in 2007 when one bad thing after another began to take place in my life despite my good works. My first thoughts were *I've sinned* and *I am being punished.* But as I reflected on my actions, I could find no sin that warranted the type and severity of "punishment" I was experiencing. Human logic was failing me yet, I spent several months condemning and beating myself up. Finally, in a moment of clarity, a still small voice whispered, "This is spiritual warfare." Armed with that truth I became mindful of the things of God and partnered with Him for an amazing journey.

This change of heart could only take place once I surrendered my belief that God's kingdom agenda was tied to a rewards system. To survive that season, I had to believe that Father knew best and that He would use my suffering to make a major impact for the kingdom.

So by the time I was diagnosed with breast cancer that same year, my inner man was ready for the fight because I *knew* God and not just knew *of* God.

Dr. Lance Watson writes, "Every person in pursuit of a dynamic and fulfilling life will be challenged by obstacles, setbacks and even tragedy." The Word tells us that a man that is born of a woman is a few days and full of trouble. Suffering happens. Period. And when you live as if your comfort is all that matters, you are selfish. Yes you read right; *you are selfish* and need to cry out to God with a heart of repentance acknowledging His sovereignty and wisdom; surrendering your will for His greater plan because it is not about you. I am not suggesting that you should neglect to pray for God's abundance in your life, but when His abundance includes some suffering, trust Him no matter what.

Here are some basic truths about how God goes about fulfilling his plan. First God is more concerned about building your character than making you happy. Second, if God only gave you what made you comfortable He would do so at the expense of others. Jesus had to suffer so that we could have life more abundantly. In turn, you may suffer for the good of others and the furthering of God's kingdom.

This life will not always be what you expect or even what you want. In fact, if you live long enough, there will come a time when God will request some things of you that you had not considered. He will present to you a set of instructions that seem so farfetched that you wonder if it is God at all. But that is how God works. Again, He isn't so much interested in your comfort as He is in building your faith. And when He is done with a situation, He wants you and others to know that it was Him and only Him who brought you through.

So now that we've gotten "you" out of the way, you can better hear what being "mindful of the things of God" looks like. The following are a list of attitudes and behaviors needed for one to be fully mindful of the things of God.

1. When you are mindful of God you are FEARLESS.
2. When you are mindful of God you are PEACEABLE.
3. When you are mindful of God you are FOCUSED/PRODUCTIVE

Keep in mind this list is not exhaustive; it's all a process. And as you surrender daily to God and His plan, completely align your heart with His through the power of the Holy Spirit you will find success and focus for your every endeavor.

WHEN YOU ARE MINDFUL OF GOD YOU ARE FEARLESS

When you are mindful of the things of God you are fearless, even at the risk of looking foolish.

It was made clear to me as a 7th grader what the first leg of my adult journey in God would look like. While browsing the library's microfilm during 4th period Study Hall, I happened upon a story of a little boy who, at the hand of an abusive parent, was killed. That story wrecked me. I instantly knew that I would become a child psychologist. How that was to be—considering I was the eldest of 8 in a working class family with no college fund—was none of my business. I just knew that it would happen because God placed that desire in my heart.

On occasion, I would verbalize my intent to become a psychologist to others. The reception was mixed; some encouraged me to pursue my goals while others, thinking I was foolish to dream so big, were skeptical. But I would not be dissuaded. I was mindful of the things of God and I knew He would do just as He had said. And He did. I became a psychologist and worked in that profession for over 10 years.

Jesus had a similar determination; not to be a psychologist, but to become Savior for all that were willing to accept Him. He knew for what purpose He had been brought to earth and He would not be tricked, bullied, or coerced to believe otherwise. So when his well-meaning disciple Peter rebuked Him for saying that He would die a criminal's death, His response, "Get behind Me, Satan!" demonstrated His strong belief in the plan God had for His life despite what others thought. In other words, Jesus was willing to look foolish. Are you?

Are you willing to risk it all and surrender your plans so that God's plan can be advanced? In life, it's easy to become mindful of the things of men rather than the things of God. The things of men tend to be logical and practical; devoid of faith and doable. While the things of God often make no earthly sense, can be terrifying and, can make us look foolish.

Case in point—Noah. It made no earthly sense that he would predict a terrible rain storm as it had never rained in such a manner. However, because Noah was mindful of the things of God and not of men, he risked ridicule and rejection to advance God's kingdom. And in the end, he was fully justified and alive.

Moses, later recognized as one of the greatest leaders that ever lived, looked quite foolish when He appeared before Pharaoh with this declaration, "This is what the LORD, the God of the Hebrews, says: 'Let my people go, so that they may worship me'". Not once but ten times! However, in the end he and the children of Israel marched out of Egypt with not only their things, but the riches of their oppressors.

Or how about the three Hebrew boys who refused to bow down to the King although they knew their disobedience would lead to an immediate and painful death? Oh yes, their response, "If that *is the case*, our God whom we serve is able to deliver us from the burning fiery furnace, and He will deliver *us* from your hand, O king. But if not, let it be known to you, O king, that we do not serve your gods, nor will we worship the gold image which you have set up" was foolish in the eyes of men. However, their faith did the impossible; they were delivered from the fire unharmed.

If you are going to pursue and succeed in the things of God, it's going to take courage. You may be rejected, talked about, and mistreated for your stance but take courage that in the end it will work out for your good! No matter what, stay fearless knowing that if God be for you who can be against you?

WHEN YOU ARE MINDFUL OF GOD YOU ARE PEACEABLE

"Behold, how good and how pleasant *it is* for brethren to dwell together in unity!" wrote King David in Psalm 133. Unfortunately, unity does not abound in the church. No; instead we would rather squabble and bicker over unimportant issues. However, when you are mindful of the things of God, you find ways to be peaceable with all men. Indeed the Word encourages us to, "Pursue peace with all *people,* and holiness, without which no one will see the Lord" (Hebrews 12:14). If you haven't seen or heard from the Lord in a long time, perhaps your level of commitment to unity is lacking.

My friend Brenda often says this statement regarding unity, "Do you want to *be* right or *do* right?" It's a great question and challenging to answer because we know that being right has its privileges and brings some level of satisfaction; however, in the end, being right and causing disunity does not bring God glory.

When you are willing to do right, (i.e., do God's will with complete devotion and little regard for your need to be right), you glorify Him in every way. Here's how. One, your willingness to take the high road shows the other person that they matter and the relationship is more important than your being right. Two, when you're willing to do right, the love of Christ is modeled in a major way through you. Imagine where we would be if Christ had decided to be right rather than do right. So out of gratitude for His sacrifice, extend the same grace to others.

Sometimes let being right and so give grace

If you are more inclined to being right than doing right, let me know how that's working for you. I would imagine not so well and that your relationships are strained and unfulfilling. Unity is the mind of God and its purpose is to allow us to work together for Him. If you are hindering the flow of unity because the world revolves around you, stop. Will yourself to do right rather than be right and watch how your relationships and circumstances change for the better.

Additionally, here are a few secrets from those who have mastered this do right thing. One, they stop holding people to impossible standards. They allow people to be human and forgive just as their Father forgives them. Two, they stop being offended by every promise broken. They acknowledge that they have broken some promises too and move on. Three, they stop cutting people off because they have a varying opinion. In other words, they surrender their right to be right and willingly do right because they are more mindful of the things of God than of men.

In January of 2000, Andel and I were engaged to be married. After setting the date, booking the venue, selecting the bridal party, ordering the bridesmaids' dresses, and sending out invitations, Andel did the unthinkable; he suggested we postpone the wedding. I was livid!

"What do you *mean* the Lord wants us to wait?" was my response to his announcement. Then before waiting for an answer, I went about laying forth every argument imaginable as to why waiting would be disastrous (I wanted to be right!). Fortunately, all of my points fell on deaf ears; Andel would not be dissuaded—he wanted to do right. So I decided in that moment that the only way to be right was to call off the engagement. Thankfully, the first person I phoned with my decision was my mother. Being the godly woman that she is, she first listened then asked, "Did he call the wedding off or did he postpone it?" I told her it was the latter. Then she spoke words that turned the entire situation around, "So if I am understanding you right, you are calling off the engagement because the man you are about to marry said that God wants you to wait." Whew, what a wake-up call. I decided to do right and we waited. I'm glad we did. Our obedience has reaped an abundant harvest of a long and satisfying marriage.

I can't imagine where I would be today if I had insisted on being right. I don't know where I would be if I had rejected Andel. God knew what was in store for me and who I needed in my life to love and support me through it all. Where would I have been without Andel's love and support while I battled cancer? How would I have left my career without his support and income? How would I have birthed our beautiful little miracles without him? God knew that I needed Andel; that our destinies were inextricably connected and I'm happy that I decided to do right rather than be right on that fateful day in June.

WHEN YOU ARE MINDFUL OF GOD YOU ARE FOCUSED/PRODUCTIVE

As a child, my favorite television show was Little House on the Prairie. Thankfully, because of re-runs my children are also able to partake in the joy I felt as a child as I watched that family relish in the simple pleasures of life. On one of the Christmas episodes, the joy of simplicity was lost on my son. As he watched Laura beam with delight over a homemade doll he stated, "One gift? What kind of Christmas is that?"

It saddens me that we've lost our way; that life has become complicated by more. Not more of God, but more things, more activities, and more distractions. For indeed our distractions have become our god, and we are more mindful of them than the true and living God who came that we might have life, and have it more abundantly.

Take a moment to consider your week. Has it been balanced, purposeful, and productive or unbalanced, chaotic, and busy? If the latter is true for you, my friend, you are not mindful of the things of God, but of men.

Today, we have no shortage of distractions from television, internet, food, and work to worries, fears, and plans. With so many things to distract us it's no wonder that so many say they can't hear God. But God is speaking and He is calling you to Him. You just have to clear the noise to hear Him; the noise the enemy has cleverly designed to be a distraction from the life God wants you to live.

But we can't blame it all on the devil; distractions serve a purpose. In other words, the person who is constantly distracted does so for a reason. So here are 3 truths about distractions that I believe will set you free. One, distractions are attractive because they are easily inserted into a life that is already overwhelmed by life. A friend of mine was overwhelmed with her family's financial situation. She turned to YouTube videos as a form of escape. She would watch these videos to the wee hours of the morning. Then when it was time for her to rise and do her morning devotions she was too tired to do so. This pattern continued for some time until she faced the truth: she was using YouTube as a distraction. Armed with that knowledge she did *The 40-Day Surrender Fast* and during that time surrendered YouTube. Her time with God proved invaluable. She gained her focus and learned to depend on God and not the computer to meet her emotional needs.

Second, distractions are dangerous because they temporarily meet a need that is crying out for a permanent solution. As it relates to the first example, my friend was temporarily relieved of the anxiety of dealing with her financial situation, but when the videos ended the problems were still there. What she needed was a permanent solution and that only comes from God.

During my undergraduate years in college, I would use all kinds of distractions to avoid the truth: I was deeply wounded and needed God for healing. In an effort to bypass God, I depended on things to fill me up. First it was books, then diet, exercise, drinking, shoplifting, anything that would give me a temporary solution. But I came to realize that these weak God-substitutes were just that—substitutes. The only One that could adequately fill and heal my hurt places was God. So I surrendered to the process of healing and am better for it today.

Third, our use of distractions is indicative of yet a larger problem: a lack of faith in God. So often we turn to distractions to divert our attention from our worries. *Will God do what He promised? I know He can do it for others, but will He do it for me?* If those thoughts sound similar to ones that you have, I want you to try this exercise from business coach, Dr. Monikah

Ogando. She says that "whatever is not worthy of God is not worthy of you" because He resides within you. If you find yourself thinking *I don't have enough money, I don't belong,* or *I will never move forward* instead of saying "I" substitute God. *God doesn't have enough money, God doesn't belong,* or *God will never move forward.* You see how ridiculous that sounds? So the next time you are thinking small recall this exercise and remember your situation is temporary, but God is eternal and there is nothing impossible with Him.

So I implore you to be mindful of the things of God and don't let distractions, doubt, fear or self-centeredness keep you from fulfilling God's plan for your life.

TWO

Surrender Is a Choice

"If anyone desires to come after Me."

Amazingly enough, following Jesus is a choice. Although He holds all power and does as He pleases (Psalm 115:3), He encourages rather than forces us to have a relationship with Him.

The first invitation to follow Him comes while we are yet sinners. When the moment is right, the Holy Spirit invites us to accept Jesus as our Lord and Savior. The process is simple—repent, acknowledge Jesus to be the Christ, and believe. Yet this simple act of faith washes us clean, makes us new in Christ, and puts us on the path to fulfilling our God-given assignment here on earth.

Repentance has two sides; it requires both a turning away from sin and turning toward God. To be truly repentant, we must do both. And without repentance we are dead in our sin and do not fully operate according to God's plan. Jesus said repeatedly in the book of John that He operated according to His father's plan and only said and did as He was instructed. If Jesus could do nothing without first consulting God, the same is most certainly true for us.

Thankfully, when you accept Christ, your spirit is made alive and you awaken to the things of God. As you grow and mature in Him, you become sensitive to His move and begin to act in ways that please Him. Through this ongoing process of sanctification, His ways become your ways and His thoughts your thoughts.

Likewise, when we accept Christ, we are imbued with power from on high in the form of the Holy Spirit. Every born-again believer has the Holy Spirit dwelling within him/her to lead and guide him/her on this journey. Jesus experienced something similar after being baptized by John the Baptist. "When He had been baptized, Jesus came up immediately from the water; and behold, the heavens were opened to Him, and He saw the Spirit of God descending like a dove and alighting upon Him. And suddenly a voice *came* from heaven, saying, "This is My beloved Son, in whom I am well pleased" (Matthew 3:16–17).

The same is true for us. When we accept Christ as our savior we are anointed with power from on high that equips us to do service for the kingdom and at conversion God accepts us just as we are and is well pleased with us. This acceptance is a product of Jesus' sacrifice, not our works. Jesus' act of love covers us and makes us well-pleasing to God.

If you are reading this book and have not accepted Jesus as your Lord and Savior, there is no better time to do so than now. Romans 10:9 reads, "That if you confess with your mouth the Lord Jesus and believe in your heart that God has raised Him from the dead, you will be saved." It's that simple. Here's a prayer to help you invite Jesus into your heart.

Heavenly Father, have mercy on me, a sinner. I believe in you and that your word is true. I believe that Jesus Christ is the Son of the living God and that he died on the cross so that I may now have forgiveness for my sins and eternal life. I know that without you in my heart my life is meaningless.

I believe in my heart that you, Lord God, raised Him from the dead. Please Jesus forgive me for every sin I have ever committed or done in my heart; please Lord Jesus forgive me and come into my heart as my personal Lord and Savior today. I need you to be my Father and my friend.

I give you my life and ask you to take full control from this moment on; I pray this in the name of Jesus Christ. Amen.

I GIVE MYSELF AWAY

Now that you've been converted, what's next? An amazing life with our Lord and Savior, that is, if you are willing to surrender all and follow Him. Sadly, just because one has chosen to accept Jesus as Savior doesn't mean that he/she has made Him Lord. To make Jesus Lord is to make Him the center, to give Him total control of your mind, will, and emotions and to sacrifice your entire being for the advancement of His kingdom.

When Jesus stated, "If any man desires to come after me," He was making several inferences. Again, the word "if" implies that desire is a choice. God is not going to force you to follow Jesus nor does He want you to follow Him out of obligation. No; instead, when we desire to come after Jesus it is something that we do willingly and from a pure heart; no hidden agendas or motivations, just a desire to be used by Him.

In Jesus' day a rich, young ruler ran to Him and asked, "Good teacher, what shall I do that I may inherit eternal life" (Mark 10:17)? Jesus commended this young man for knowing all of the law, but encouraged him to do something he would not; "One thing you lack: go your way, sell whatever you have and give to the poor, and you will have treasure in heaven; and come, take up the cross, and follow Me." The young man went away very sorrowful because he was unwilling to part with his riches and to give himself away.

Perhaps leaving riches is not your issue, but we all have something that tempts us to follow "it" instead of God. That's why the Word demands that we choose this day who we will serve. Will it be God or mammon?

Some say that following Jesus today is more challenging than ever; that the opposition against Christians is so great that it is safer to blend in and serve Jesus privately then to be a bold, fearless Christian with a message. Sure, blending is easier, but it is by no means the safe choice. Matthew 10:33 reminds us, "But whoever denies Me before men, him I will also deny before My Father who is in heaven."

I am not negating the fact that there is great opposition, but every person before you and every person after you who decides to make Jesus his/

her choice has faced and will face opposition. Who faced greater opposition than Daniel? In his day, any man who was found serving or worshipping anyone besides the king would be put into a Lion's Den. What did Daniel do? Three times a day he worshipped God anyway and in plain sight! His behavior was reported to the king and he was thrown into the Lion's Den. But God, who has all power, shut the jaws of the lions and the mouths of Daniel's haters. The next morning Daniel was retrieved from the den unharmed and his enemies received the punishment they had sought for him.

It is my belief that when you truly desire to come after Jesus you take a stand for Him and righteousness no matter what. You don't just simply drift along with whatever is pleasant and easy, but you purpose in your heart that for God you live and for God you die.

In I Kings 18:21, the prophet Elijah asked those in the assembly, "How long will you falter between two opinions? If the Lord *is* God, follow Him; but if Baal, follow him." Today rather than stone or wood we value power, status, appearance, and/or material possessions. These gods are dangerous because they cause us to depend more on them than the living God.

However, when the challenges of life weigh us down we quickly learn that those substitute gods are just that—substitutes, and completely incapable of giving us life more abundantly.

Take a moment to reflect on your life and more importantly your choices and decisions. Are you doing what is pleasing to God or pleasing to your flesh? The things we value we devote time and energy to and anything we exalt above God becomes an idol. In fact, when we esteem anything more than God we have made that thing a god. Therefore, if you are drifting through life doing what pleases your flesh, the false god you will discover you are worshiping is yourself.

Popular songs of today include, "I Give Myself Away," and "I Surrender All", but how many of those who sing these songs really mean it? How many have counted the cost and still say yes? The young ruler certainly had not counted the cost before he approached Jesus. His motives seemed pure on the surface however, when probed it was evident that he was unwilling to put God at the center; he was unwilling to focus on something other than his agenda, his plans, and his self-preservation.

In a society that glorifies the pursuit of things, it is easy to lose focus and go about God's business from a selfish posture. Therefore, today and every day be intentional about choosing Jesus. Pray as David did, "Search me, O God, and know my heart; try me, and know my anxieties; and see if *there is any* wicked way in me, and lead me in the way everlasting" (Psalm 139:23–24). Dying to yourself daily and having a heart of surrender will allow you to give yourself away to Jesus no matter what is required.

THE INVITATION TO MORE

I'll let you in on a little secret. Responding "yes" to the call of the Lord opens you to more. Not just more opposition, as some fear, but more love, peace, joy, and abundance. The God who daily loads you with benefits is waiting on you to surrender and say yes to Him. When you open yourself to Him and respond in obedience to His call you open yourself to more blessings than you could ever imagine. Deuteronomy 28:1 reminds us that if we diligently harken to the voice of the Lord that He will overtake us with the blessings. I don't know about you, but I don't mind being consumed by God's blessings.

Don't misconstrue what I am trying to convey. Indeed, we follow Jesus because we love Him and it's the right thing to do. However, following Him also has it benefits. It's funny; my friend Joy says that obedience is God's love language. I tend to agree. There are numerous instances in the Bible of Jesus inviting others to follow Him and when they did so their act of obedience opened them to more.

Abraham and Peter are just two examples of how obedience allows God to do exceedingly, abundantly above all we can ask or think. Abraham was called to leave all that he knew and to do so without further instructions. Because His desire for God was greater than his desire for comfort, he made himself eligible for this promise, "I will make you exceedingly fruitful; and I will make nations of you, and kings shall come from you" (Genesis 17:6).

Peter appeared perfectly content with his small-town fishing job, but when Jesus invited him to become a fisher "of men" he responded with a yes and that yes made him privy to this promise, "you are Peter, and on this rock I will build My church, and the gates of Hades shall not prevail against it" (Matthew 16:18).

What is God calling you to? Will you desire Him more than anything? I am a living witness that a yes opens you to more than you can ask or think. Your yes will make you privy to the beyond, beyond blessings of God. And your yes will transcend you to bless your children and your children's children. Just give Him all!

WHEN SAYING "YES" IS HARD

I hear you saying, "Celeste, all of that is easier said than done." Indeed it's easier said, but it can be done. Over the years, I have learned to say "yes" quickly. It wasn't always that way. In the beginning I debated, asked other's opinions, and downright refused to obey God, but as He proved Himself over and over again I gained confidence in His ability to do the impossible. Additionally, I heard a pastor say that the space between hearing God and saying yes is the space you give the enemy time to convince you that no is the right answer or to convince you to do part of what God is calling you to do. Let me remind you that partial obedience is still disobedience. In God's economy, you don't get partial credit for doing half of what he has called you to do. He wants your full obedience.

I am a living witness that responding with a "yes" isn't always easy. In 2008, while at a Christmas party, I heard a most unusual story of faith from a remarkable couple that attends my church. In short, they both left their military positions just years from retirement to pursue full-time ministry at the church. Soon after the sharing of their stories I heard the Lord instruct me to leave all that I knew: private practice, speaking, ministry positions, everything!

Needless to say, I was shocked. On the way home I decided to mention to Andel what I believed the Lord was saying to me. I thought, *surely he won't agree* as he had declared from our engagement that we would always be a two-income family. But Andel's response to my disclosure was the second shocker of the night. "If you believe that God is saying that to you, then do it". With that I was assured that God had spoken and I complied with His request albeit challenging.

Therefore, for all of 2009, I went about releasing myself from every obligation: private practice, speaking, ministry positions, writing, as I prepared to go to a place the Lord would show me. I soon found out that place was my home. Unfortunately, for the first 3 months or so I was double-minded. In one breath I thanked God for the opportunity to take this amazing journey with Him, but no sooner did I have that thought, I confessed how miserable I was to be sitting home. Responding with a "yes" was not easy for me, but God was patient.

It wasn't until April of that same year that I surrendered. It was then that God instructed me to do a spiritual fast for 40 days. I knew what I had to surrender: my diet. For years the Holy Spirit had been urging me to clean up my diet and although I knew the link between diet and disease I continued to eat poorly. In fact, I was the biggest junk food junkie. However, I answered the call with a yes and did what most know to be the Daniel Fast. It was very difficult; although I was not hungry, for the first couple of weeks I stayed in a constant state of dissatisfaction. Therefore, every day of that Surrender Fast I had to depend on God and pray with fervor, "Lord help me to crave the foods that are good for me." To my surprise, around day 30 or so I realized that God had changed my palette in such a way that I no longer desired to eat meat and have been a vegetarian ever since.

Then on the heels of the first fast, God instructed me to fast again. This time not from food, but from selfishness. So for 40 days I served my family unselfishly. Not many days after that fast ended, the Lord asked me to fast one last time in 2010, but this time He wanted me to ask others to fast with me. I was scared. I have this thing about rejection and would much rather assume a "no" than to give someone the opportunity to say no to me. However, because I desired to "come after God", I showed up with a "yes" and the rest is history. About 100 of us fasted, each surrendering something different as unto the Lord. To keep us connected I posted to a blog each day. Little did I know that in 40 days time I had written a book known now as *The 40-Day Surrender Fast*. Little did I know that showing up with a "yes" no matter how challenging, would change the lives of those around me and the lives of people for generations to come.

It is evident from my story that saying yes wasn't easy; however, because I showed up with a yes God showed up with so much more. Through my obedience others have been released to their earthly ministries, marriages have been restored, debt has been cancelled, and many have been physically healed.

Imagine what your yes could accomplish. As the Word tells us in Proverbs 16:9, "A man's heart plans his way, but the Lord directs his steps." You are also encouraged to trust in the Lord with all your heart and lean not to your own understanding. Although you may not understand why God is directing you to take a certain road or make a certain decision, trust Him. He knows what He is doing and has plans to prosper you and bring you to an expected end. Just come after Him with all your heart.

THREE

Surrender Reveals the Real Me

"Let Him Deny Himself."

As if the surrendering of desires and agenda isn't challenging enough for the average Christian, Jesus goes further and tacks on self-denial. At first glance, desire for Jesus and self-denial may appear to be one in the same; however, denial of self can only occur after we desire to follow after Jesus with our whole heart. It is from this sincere place of desire that our actions take on a selfless nature and conform to the will of God.

In a society that promotes individualism over collectivism and is seemingly obsessed with the idea of meeting one's own needs, self-denial sounds foreign, ridiculous in fact. With popular phrases like, "it's all about you, have it your way, and it's just me, myself and I" we are encouraged to focus on ourselves and meet our own needs at any cost.

But what is self-absorption really about? Is it that we've become egotistical beyond measure or are we covering for a deeper problem? Oftentimes it's the latter. In fact, self-denial and selflessness are difficult to obtain when we have issues of the heart. Thankfully, the process of surrender creates in us a clean heart and reveals our true self. In this section, we will focus on the re-education of the selfish Christian. I know that's not you, it's your neighbor, but just read along so that you know how to disciple him/her when the time comes. In the meantime, let's explore 3 conditions of the heart that make self-denial impossible: the Self-Centered Heart, the Wounded Heart, and the Distrustful Heart.

THE SELF-CENTERED HEART

According to Merriam-Webster Dictionary, selfishness is having or showing concern only for yourself and not for the needs or feelings of other people. In fact, when we are selfish we become the center of our universe. And when we are at the center, God can't be.

Being self-centered is both innate and learned. Just watch children at play. Even with a limited vocabulary they know the word "mine." This tendency to be self-centered, especially if reinforced, typically carries on into adulthood. In fact, the word "mine" is alive and well in our marriages, workplaces, and sadly, even in the church. Don't believe me? Try to sit in Sister So and So's seat next week. You may just have a fight on your hands!

Where I am today is a product of my willingness to be selfless. Not that I'm good at it, for indeed I am self-centered by nature. You would think being raised in a family of 10 would have squashed any selfishness that was in me, but indeed it didn't. So the fact that God entrusted to me the ministry of surrender shows He has a sense of humor and His grace is unfailing.

When I look out on the landscape of servanthood in the church, I find that some of God's children are serving for their own gain and not His. The quality of their life is poor because of their self-centeredness. They are scattered, tired, and in some cases burned out. They are all things to all people, but no good for themselves or God. In the end, their work will be rejected. Jesus said in Matthew 7:22–23, "Many will say to Me in that day, 'Lord, Lord, have we not prophesied in Your name, cast out demons in Your name, and done many wonders in Your name?' And then I will declare to them, 'I never knew you; depart from Me, you who practice lawlessness!'"

Indeed, when you serve from an impure or self-centered heart you are practicing lawlessness. In other words, you are rebelling against God. And this should not be so. Therefore, as you transition from self-centered to selfless, purpose in your heart to one, stop playing "god" to feed your ego and two, say "no" to some opportunities so that others are allowed a chance to do God's work.

From Self-Centered to Selfless

Again, putting God at the center has been and continues to be challenging for me. I am most aware of this challenge when I am involved in ministry. I've learned that there is a fine line between a desire to advance God's kingdom and my own. Maybe you can relate. Even well-meaning Christian leaders cross this line and/or go back and forth without conscious knowledge of doing so. But if we are going to truly do God's work we will have to deny ourselves daily and be selfless.

When God is at the center, we no longer focus on our agenda, our plans, and our self-preservation. Instead, our focus becomes kingdom-driven. Over the last couple of years whenever I find myself in a space of aggravation, frustration, and anxiousness, I can hear the Holy Spirit whispering, "So whose agenda are you doing?" That brief yet powerful statement jolts me from a self-focus to a God-focus. Indeed, when I am pursuing the things of God I am at peace in my mind, and have a sense of being "at rest" although I may be juggling several assignments. I've learned that when I am propelled by grace, there is no limit to what God can do in and through me.

So how does God change a self-centered heart to a selfless one? Through our experiences. As God transforms us, He calls us to a place of discomfort, a place where we are encouraged to put others first, to be sacrificial, even when it looks as if we might lose.

Queen Esther in the Bible is a prime example of going from self-centered to selfless. As the story goes, she was appointed queen after the de-throning of Queen Vashti by King Ahasuerus. If Esther had her way that would have been the end of the story; she would have been content to be the queen. However, she wasn't appointed by man but God and He had a plan for her life. After learning that her people, the Jews, were slated for annihilation, she had a tough decision to make: go on with life as usual or risk her life for the safety of her people. It wasn't an easy choice; everything in her was screaming "Be self-centered!" She was young, pretty, and rich, but she realized that fulfilling the Lord's call was more important than pushing her own agenda, so she chose the road less traveled; the road of selflessness and was quoted thus,

"I will go to the king, which *is* against the law; and if I perish, I perish!" God changed her heart as only He can, and she has been credited with saving her people, the Jews, from annihilation through her act of selflessness.

Take a page from my own life. Making the decision to close my private practice in 2009 was a major sacrifice for my family; we were risking a great deal. At the time I was called to do this we were on one income as Andel was unemployed. He had recently retired from the military and was yet to be employed. Despite that reality, God instructed me to leave it all. From my experience, God often directs me to make a sacrifice when it's inconvenient (I guess that's why it's called a sacrifice). Nonetheless, I've also learned that when you follow His plan you can't go wrong.

So we decided not to let Andel's unemployment influence our decision. We would obey God no matter what. Then the impossible happened. Just days after our radical yes, Andel received 3 job offers! Not only would he work, he could choose which job was best. God can do exceedingly, above all you can think. Surrender advanced us and it will advance you. You can't lose when God is in it and your selfless acts will reap an abundant harvest.

Another great example of serving from a selfless posture is when you do so while in a troubled marriage. Perhaps you've been called to be the sacrificial lamb in your marriage although your spouse is in the wrong and/or has satisfied the requirements for you to leave. Sure the Bible gives allowance for divorce when a spouse is unfaithful, however is being unfaithful a guaranteed exit from a painful marriage? That's between you and God. The Word tells us in all your ways acknowledge Him and He shall direct your paths (Proverbs 3:6).

Be as Jesus was with Peter in Matthew 16:23 and don't let popular opinion direct your steps. Have you considered that perhaps God wants to use you as a vessel of healing for that wayward spouse? He may want to demonstrate His unconditional love in a big way through you.

Hosea was called to this demonstration of God's love. In the book of Hosea, he was instructed, "Go, take to yourself a wife of harlotry, and have children of harlotry; for the land commits flagrant harlotry, forsaking the Lord" (Hos. 1:2). You think God won't call you to a challenging situation? Think again. God is not in the business of making you comfortable and happy, but in the business of advancing His kingdom through surrendered/selfless people like you.

THE WOUNDED HEART

Contrary to popular belief, selfishness is not simply a product of being "spoiled". Selfishness is also learned through offense and often times we are self-centered because we have been hurt. When one has been hurt and has not dealt properly with the hurt, there is a tendency for that person to become the center of his/her universe. For this reason, we must actively choose to put off offense and continue to give God first place in every area of our heart, especially our hurt places.

Again, my story of surrender is relevant here. As mentioned, in 2010 God required of me a selflessness that defied logic. He asked me to surrender all of my activities to Him *including ministry*. At the time, surrendering "worldly" activities—like writing and public speaking—made sense, but ministry? *Wasn't that God's work?*

Hoping that God would change His mind, I waited till the 11th hour to tell my First Lady that I was to resign from my ministry position as leader of Women's Focus Studies. I later came to understand that surrendering ministry was so challenging because being involved in ministry filled voids in my heart I wasn't consciously aware that I had. But God knew and was calling me to a higher place in Him; a place where ministry could no longer be a substitute for Him. So often we are doing God's work without allowing His work to be done in us. Therefore, when God says "you shall have no other god before me," He means it. And if ministry has become your god, He will remove it. Beloved, God does not want you to define yourself by your title, role, or status, but by who you are in Him. No matter what you are doing, the fact that you are His, gives you purpose.

I didn't know all of this those many years ago when I was attempting to negotiate with God to keep my ministry position. Boy, did I plead. I went from *God the women need me, and I want to advance Your kingdom,* to *if you make me give this up I'll miss the leadership retreats and won't be able to hang out with the First Lady and the other ministry leaders at her home.* But no matter how I begged, God was not budging. So in a last ditch effort of desperation I cried out, "God you are making me a NOBODY!"

Where had that come from? I know. It came from a broken place in my heart that God knew was there from childhood. Sadly, I had been using ministry to fill my own need: the need to belong, to be loved, and esteemed. Not that those needs are wrong, for they are inherent in every human being, but those needs are to be met by God and not from a leadership position.

However, before you go judging me, consider this. How many of us do God's work for the perks of the work and not the love of the work? Don't get me wrong; there was a part of me that loved the work, but if the love of the work and doing God's will was all there was to it, when He said leave, I would have responded with an immediate "yes". Jesus said over and over again in the book of John phrases akin to *I only said and did what my Father told me to say and do.* When God said enough, it's over, move on, Jesus said "yes." You know why? Because Jesus was about His Father's business and His identity wasn't wrapped up in what He was doing, but in Who He was doing it for.

So again from a place of woundedness I selfishly clung to ministry. I needed ministry to survive, but I finally surrendered and the rest is history. God moved me on to my next assignment in Him and placed in my stead a phenomenal leader who took the ministry to new heights for Him.

If you sense the call of God to move and you are refusing, check the condition of your heart, ask God to 'show you you' and allow Him to minister to your hurt places. Then you'll be ready to be used by Him in a most amazing way.

THE DISTRUSTFUL HEART

As I close this chapter, I can hear some of you saying *I am far from selfish, I am the person everyone comes to in time of need.* If that's you, let's explore the heart behind your serving for indeed you are either working for the Lord or working for yourself.

To have a servant's heart and a commitment to serving God's people is God's will. Matthew 23:11 reads, "The greatest among you will be a servant." John 12:26 reminds us, "If anyone serves Me, let him follow Me; and where I am, there My servant will be also. If anyone serves Me, him *My* Father will honor." So how do you know the difference between serving for God and serving for your own selfish needs or gain? I am glad you asked.

First and foremost, God needs you to serve Him. When you learn to serve Him then and only then are you ready to truly serve others. Serving God means doing as He commands and willingly following His instructions—in other words, surrendering to His Lordship in the area of service. Sometimes this can be challenging especially when you haven't learned to trust the Lord. This distrust of God is usually a direct result of being wounded by significant others in childhood. When these god-figures, whom you see, break your trust it becomes exponentially more challenging to trust a God you have not seen. But indeed He can be trusted.

First, God is for you and you don't have to play God. The martyr attitude of *let's-take-one-for-the-team* and *I-can-be-all-things-to-all-people-even-when-I-have-no-more-to-give* is rooted in distrust. You don't trust God to do it for you and you don't trust that He will do it for others. But again, for that reason you are tired, drained, and unfulfilled. Your relationship with God suffers and you are far from fulfilling the call God has on your life.

When we play God, we demonstrate our lack of trust in Him; we are essentially telling God that we can do it better. And not only are we "doing it better" for ourselves—NOT—we are dragging others into our foolishness. But I tell you today that when you play God because you don't trust Him and in turn play god for other people you are being the worst kind of selfish. Thankfully, there is a better way and that way is surrender.

Second, when you stop playing God you will free others to be all that they are to be in Him. I told you earlier in this chapter that if I had not heeded God's command to leave my ministry leadership role I would have hindered the next (ordained and anointed) person from filling that role. In fact, in the body God has a role for all of us. We are all members of one body. He is not requiring you to be all of the members, just one maybe two. So if you are trying to be all things to all people, "*go somewhere and sit down!*" as the young people would say.

Indeed, "sitting down" is for the good of the church, the good of the kingdom and for your own good. The Word tells you to love your neighbor as you love yourself. When you love yourself, you make sure to make yourself a priority so that you are good for others. I tell you what. I dare you to die tomorrow and come back as a spectator. Guess what? People will move on—almost immediately.

Think about it. Is being the center of everyone else's universe worth your losing your destiny? I suspect the answer is no. If trusting in God is an issue for you, may I suggest that you "try" God as He challenges us in Malachi. As the Word tells us, He will never leave you nor forsake you, His love is everlasting, and He is a light unto your feet. So much so that He sends His angels of protection to hold you up with their hands so you won't even hurt your foot on a stone. Who wouldn't serve a God like that?

Therefore, as you walk through the process of denying yourself, let God use you as He sees fit to serve His people, to fulfill your call, and to give Him glory. Then and only then will the real you be revealed.

FOUR

Surrender Requires Death

"Take up your cross."

W hat does it mean to take up one's cross? Well
let's start with what it doesn't mean. Many
well-meaning Christians take the cross to mean some
type of suffering, loss of a job or loved one, disease
or the bearing of a hardship for the Lord, but there is
a deeper meaning if we consider the context. When
Jesus carried His cross to Golgotha to be crucified,
it was not a symbolic cross; He wasn't carrying some
personal burden. No, He was carrying a literal cross
which would be instrumental in His literal death by
execution in one of the most painful and humiliating

ways humans of the 1st century could think to kill a person.

So when Jesus asks you to take up your cross He isn't calling you to a suffering party, but to something far more challenging. He is calling you to die and more specifically to die to self. The Word tells us "precious in the sight of the Lord is the death of His saints" (Psalms 116:15). Likewise, taking up your cross is not necessarily an implication of death in the physical sense, but death of self and death of your will. It's an opportunity to live selflessly and humbly. When you surrender to the cross experience, you nail your flesh and all its fleshly ideas to the cross so that His will can be made manifest in your life.

In the context of Matthew 16:24, to die is to give your whole life and being to the Lord, as He gave His life for us. Not just a one-time surrender in order to receive salvation, but a daily dying of self through sanctification and repentance. Therefore, it is with authority that Jesus can speak of taking up a cross because He took up His own. He who knew no wrong died for all wrong. Thankfully, in His cross experience He not only saved us from eternal damnation, He taught us valuable lessons on how we can successfully take up our own crosses.

CRUCIFIED WITH CHRIST

The apostle Paul wrote in Galatians 2:20, "I have been crucified with Christ; it is no longer I who live, but Christ lives in me; and the life which I now live in the flesh I live by faith in the Son of God, who loved me and gave Himself for me." What better way to honor that sacrifice than to give of ourselves sacrificially? To die to self and the flesh.

The flesh is weak, limited, and temporal. Being crucified with Christ means we no longer follow the flesh and its desires, but depend wholly on Jesus for guidance, direction, and comfort. When the flesh has been crucified we acknowledge God in all our ways and no longer put our trust in man or ourselves, but in the Father. Every dream, ambition, and desire needs to be re-evaluated and those found to be in opposition to God's will, must be nailed to the cross. The process of crucifying the flesh is not for the faint at heart. Many a believer has failed to surrender all when the "all" involved doing, saying, or being something other than what they thought was part of the plan they had devised for their lives. Did you catch that? The plan *they* had devised. The plan that says, *my will, my way*, but that's not true surrender. True surrender, as so eloquently put by Tyra Lane Kingsland, author and speaker is *"His will, His way!"*

What aspect of the flesh do you need to kill today? What ideas, thoughts, dreams, and ambitions are keeping you from being all that you can be in Christ? Not that these are wrong but anything you exalt over God must die. Perhaps it's an overwhelming desire to be married, an obsession with obtaining the perfect body, a great drive for accomplishments, or an insatiable desire for material possessions. Whatever that might be for you, put it under the scrutiny of the Holy Spirit and let those things die in you.

Indeed, the way of the cross is the only way to acquire a life worth living and to not only live, but to live more abundantly. Thankfully, it is from Christ's cross experience (his arrest, trial and crucifixion) that we can learn how to successfully take up our own crosses and come to a place of complete surrender in Him.

Step #1—Arrest Your Flesh.

Just as Jesus was arrested in the Garden of Gethsemane after a long night of prayer, so must your flesh be put under arrest and be required to surrender to the plans and thoughts of our Lord and Savior. As you seek God in prayer and fasting, the Spirit will reveal to you the thoughts, plans, and behaviors that are not of Him. As He does that, arrest those fleshly behaviors so that they no longer have a place in your life.

Step #2—Put Your Flesh on Trial.

Just as Jesus stood before Pontius Pilate, so must your flesh stand before the Lord with the Holy Spirit being the judge and jury. As you surrender and allow the cross experience to happen in your being, every dream and desire that originates with you will be found guilty and sentenced to death.

Step #3—Execution of the Flesh.

Just as Jesus carried His cross to Golgotha, so must you carry your cross to its place of execution. It will be a long road filled with grueling work, but necessary for the fulfillment of your call and the advancement of God's kingdom. The process of death will be challenging, you will want to ask for a pardon. But as Jesus did, carry your cross to the place of execution and willingly die so that Christ may live in your life.

MY EVERYTHING

The apostle Paul is an excellent example of what it means to die to self and live selflessly. In Romans 1:1, he opens his letter to the church in Rome with this profoundly humble introduction, "Paul, a bondservant of Jesus Christ, called *to be* an apostle, separated to the gospel of God." In this, Paul willingly identifies himself as a servant and apostle sent by Jesus to spread the gospel. His words aren't to be taken lightly or dismissed easily. As a Roman citizen, it was beneath him to call himself a servant. In fact, to call oneself anything akin to a servant was unthinkable. However, in this brief phrase Paul demonstrated that he had died to himself and was willing to be nothing so that Jesus could be his all and all.

Jesus became a servant to be our all and all too. Philippians 2:8 reads, "Who, being in the form of God, did not consider it robbery to be equal with God, but made Himself of no reputation, taking the form of a bondservant, *and* coming in the likeness of men. And being found in appearance as a man, He humbled Himself and became obedient to *the point of* death, even the death of the cross."

Jesus and Paul demonstrate that with death comes life. Likewise, your death to the flesh will not be in vain; it will produce fruit and such fruit being humility. In *Humility*, author Andrew Murray writes that humility is the place of total dependence on God. He further writes, "Humility is not a thing we bring to God. It is also not a thing God gives to us. It is simply the realization of what nothings we really are, when we truly see how God is Everything, and when we clear out room in our hearts so that He can be everything for us."

I certainly want God to be "my everything", but I must admit that every time I read of Paul describing himself as a servant and in some translations a slave, my spirit is slightly vexed. It's such a strong word and considering that I am a descendent of slaves, it's not a position/posture I readily embrace. However, if I am going to effectively advance God's kingdom agenda, I will have to get over the semantics and willingly be nothing to a God that is everything.

In ancient Jewish culture, being nothing was demonstrated in a profound way via the interaction between rabbi and student. In this culture, formal education began at the age of 6 for boys. The exceptional ones advanced on into *bet midrash* ("house of study"), the final phase of his formal education. Applicants asked a local rabbi if they could be his *talmidim* ("disciples"). If chosen, they were invited to follow the rabbi. This wasn't a check in once-a-week-for-supervision type of follow. No, this was an I-give-up-my-whole-life-to-be-like-the-rabbi type of follow. In turn, the student spent every waking moment with the rabbi, learning his philosophy and following his practices. It was complete devotion and total surrender as they only said, thought and did like the rabbi.

What would happen for us if we decided to be completely devoted to Christ? How much more could we live the abundant life He promised if we would just abide in Him? Rabbis are human; they are flawed and prone to mistakes but Christ is none of those things; He is perfect. So following Him can be without fear as following Him brings life and it is for that reason we die knowing that our death brings life!

LOVE ME MORE THAN THESE?

There is no lasting fulfillment without God. In fact we, in and of ourselves, are not enough for ourselves or anyone else; wholeness only comes from Him. People can't fill us, things can't fill us; the only thing that can fill us is the life that comes from God and the only way to be eligible for that life is to lose the one we've created. If anyone tells you that you can achieve greatness without dying, their message is from Satan. There is no other way to complete God's greater dream for your life than to die.

In John 21:15, Peter was challenged to lose His life with these words:

> "Simon, *son* of Jonah, do you love Me more than these?" He said to Him, "Yes, Lord; You know that I love You." He said to him, "Feed My lambs."

There are a few things to note about this invitation. First, the request to lose your life always starts with a question that seeks to answer, "Do you love me more than these?" Peter was quite offended by this question, but Jesus knew it was necessary for Him to test Peter's alliance in this way. Likewise, whenever you make a declaration of love unto the Lord, don't be surprised when your sincerity is called into question. It is necessary because if truth be told, if you don't lose your life to Jesus, something else will find your allegiance. The Word tells us in Matthew 6:21, "For where your treasure is, there your heart will be also." God knows the condition of your heart and it is through the process of surrender that you, too, come to know its condition.

Second, the invitation to lose one's life is a choice. You are free to respond to this invitation any way you like. God is not going to force you to follow Him. Although He knows your life won't really start until you choose Him, He gives us freewill to choose our own path.

Many years ago, when I was just a little girl, my mother attended a church service. When the invitation to accept Christ was made, she sensed the Lord leading her to give her life to Him. She had sensed this call several times before, but had refused the invitation as she was unwilling to jeopardize her relationship with her unsaved husband. So this time, like the others, she wrestled with losing her life to follow Jesus, but this time, unlike the others, she said yes and declared through action, that no one was more important than God. When she announced to my dad what she had done, he laughed. When she told her close friends, they laughed too. But not for long. Within that year, they all accepted Christ as their Savior. Her love for God was clear; they sensed it, and wanted to know God too.

DEATH AT CONVERSION WAS
JUST THE BEGINNING

When you accept Jesus as your Lord and Savior, at conversion you willingly die to the old self and are created new in Christ. However, that death is not the end, but the beginning of a series of deaths that should occur throughout your walk with Christ.

It is important to note that the conversion death or process of salvation may well be the easiest of all the deaths you'll experience as a Christian because that death is all about you. You are the focus and your acceptance of Christ makes eternal life guaranteed. Salvation occurs in an instant; however, the process of sanctification is ongoing and requires death to self on a daily basis. This daily submission to death is not easy as it requires you to do so at your own expense and for the greater good. In this *all-about-me-world* no wonder many Christians refuse to continue to the process of death after conversion. They are too busy living as if this life is all about them, but Christ is calling us to die in order to find the life He intended from the beginning.

Paul wrote that he died daily. To die daily is to wake with a renewed mind to surrender all to Christ; to resist temptation and to walk uprightly. We are more than capable of doing this as God daily loads us with benefits and empowers us to do better, be better, and live better.

The thought of dying daily might be overwhelming for you. *Isn't accepting Christ enough?* Yes and no.

Accepting Christ will get you into heaven, but dying to the life you've built for the one He intended, will bring heaven to you on earth. While death is necessary God, in His mercy, moves at our pace. As a babe in Christ, it is unlikely that God will call you to quit your job and move to another country. No; rather He allows us to take baby steps, building us up for the next sacrificial death that will advance His kingdom.

Think about it. The great men of the Bible advanced slowly too. They complied with God's call to die one invitation at a time. Each call to die challenged their faith the more; each call got them closer and closer to greater. Abraham would have been unwilling to sacrifice Isaac, the son of the promise, had he not left all to follow God to an unknown place. Daniel would have been unable to open himself to death via the Lion's Den had he not said "no" to the king's delicacies, and Joseph would have been unwilling to forgive his brothers had he not allowed God to empower him to forgive the other people who had betrayed him along the way. These men had to die to gain and so will you. The following are specific ways in which God requires us to die:

1. Death of Plans

I've always been a planner. In my teens and early twenties I prided myself on being the master of my destiny. Whatever I thought—was. Whatever I wanted—happened, or so I liked to think.

I knew I would be a psychologist, that I would go to college tuition-free, be married by 30, and have two children: a boy, and a girl, in that order. All of it happened just like that. So imagine my surprise when I was diagnosed with breast cancer in 2007. That wasn't in my plans. However, it was from this and other experiences that I've learned that the only thing that is sure is God's Word. Forget about what you want; if it is not in His will, it's all for naught.

There is nothing wrong with planning; however, when planning comes from a place of fear or is about maintaining control, it is not from God. Rather than living by faith we live by sight. Rather than asking God what He has planned we ask Him to fit into our plans. I heard a preacher say that if you want to make God laugh, share with Him your plans.

I am sure God has gotten many a laugh from me. Case in point; Andel and I married while I was in graduate school. In fact, it was my last year. In order to complete my doctorate program I was required to complete a year-long internship. It didn't matter where, as long as it got done. But for me the "where" mattered. I needed Maryland, DC, or Virginia because there was no way I was going to leave my newly married, handsome husband all alone in an area where the women outnumbered the men. So I went about applying exclusively to internships in these areas. Not once did I ask God was this His plan; I only prayed that He would make it so. His Will, my way, right? Well, imagine my disappointment when none of the 9 internships I applied to accepted me.

I immediately called my normally mild-mannered father for some sympathy. He was completely sympathetic until I declared that I was "trying not to be mad at God." He reprimanded me in a way that surprised and hurt me. But it caused me to think. He was right; God had done nothing wrong. It was my fear that had gotten me into this mess.

So the next day I went about finding another potential internship among the few internship programs that had not matched to a candidate. The first internship that popped up was an internship in Chicago. What most intrigued me was that this internship was Christian-based and the job description fit me to a tee. *How had I missed this?* Oh right. I only wanted to be in Maryland, DC, or Virginia; however God had another plan. As I spoke with the director, he stated a phrase that will forever stick with me, "you are an answer to prayer." I am thankful that God found me worthy enough to be an answer to someone else's prayer even after messing up so badly.

As this story indicates, because I was willing to forego my plan for God's, He made the way straight. But that's not the end of the story. Just a few weeks after obtaining the internship, my sister was hired by a major airline and thus granted flying privileges. She and her husband decided that they would grant me the opportunity to fly instead of him. So for the entire year that I was in Chicago I flew to Maryland (for free) every weekend to be with my husband. We serve an amazing God!

If you are holding your plans tight in an effort to maintain control, stop. You are not in control and you won't start living your best life until you surrender it all to God. Again there is nothing wrong with planning, but we are to allow some room for the manifestation of God's will when it doesn't line up with our own. God's kingdom agenda needs freedom to advance without our preconceived notions of how and when He should do it. We are vessels to be used by Him; clay in the Master's hands to be formed as He chooses.

When God is the center of our lives, His plans become our plans. His will becomes our will. We are no longer pushing our agenda, but acknowledging Him in all our ways even down to the minutest thing. However, when we are self-directed and leave God out of the equation, fear directs our decision-making. Our plans include contingencies and we make allowances for our mistakes by formulating back up plans B, C and D.

God's plans for us on the other hand, which are a product of His extraordinary love, have no need to be altered or fixed by us. You'll discover as you learn to master the art of surrender that there is no need for a Plan B because God is perfect and His will for us is perfect. That's why Jesus rebuked Peter so severely about His death because Peter was operating from the fleshly need to avoid pain whereas Jesus was willing to accept pain for the greater good of all.

So as you learn to surrender and die to yourself and your plans, a very important question to ponder is, "Are my plans God-driven or self-driven?" Sometimes it's hard to tell the difference. If you are anything like me you are full of ideas. Some of my ideas are good ideas while others are God ideas. Here's how I gauge the difference. First, I give the idea some time to marinate; I don't jump right on it and get to making it happen. I've learned that the passion for my good idea fades relatively quickly (usually within days, sometimes hours) while the God idea won't let me rest. Second, a God idea is often confirmed through scripture or in a conversation with another person. I've known and believed for some time that I am an International Healing Ministry. Just recently, while speaking at a church, it dropped in my spirit that I was released. I stood before the church and told them that I am an International Healing Ministry. The pastor in turn confirmed this to be true by saying that I was released to international ministry from her pulpit. The very next day, I received a letter from a Bishop in Kenya inviting me to speak at their Pastors and Leaders Conference the following year!

Bottom line: hold your plans loosely. Don't be hasty. Move as God says move in the time that He gives you to move and be willing to let die those dreams and ideas that are not of Him. I am a living witness that when you do so, greater comes.

2. Death of Relationships

Let's face it; some relationships last a lifetime while others are seasonal. The wisdom to know the difference comes from God. In the book of Ruth, after Naomi had lost her husband and two sons, she urged her daughters-in-law to return to their country of origin. Orpah complied, but Ruth would not be persuaded. In Ruth 1: 16–17 we read,

But Ruth said: "Entreat me not to leave you,
Or to turn back from following after you;
For wherever you go, I will go;
And wherever you lodge, I will lodge;
Your people *shall be* my people,
And your God, my God.

Where you die, I will die,
And there will I be buried.
The LORD do so to me, and more also,
If *anything but* death parts you and me."

I guess Ruth was determined to be a friend for life! In fact, she had to be; their destinies were intricately tied. Orpah, on the other hand wasn't a flake; she just understood that their season had ended.

Ironically, as I write this section of the book, I am dealing with a series of dying relationships. If they were ending for an apparent reason, like in the story of Ruth that would be fine. But these relationships are ending for no obvious reason and that is challenging for me. Nonetheless, I am learning not everyone can go where God is taking me. I am also learning that God will move those from my path that are not for me. And the same is true for you. You can't take everyone where you are going. If someone doesn't like you, shake the dust off your feet and move on. You weren't designed to go where they are going and they weren't designed to go where you are going. Thankfully, as we allow God to remove the relationships that are not ordained by Him, we make room for His divine connections.

3. Death of a False Identity

Identity is the fact of being who or what a person or thing is. If asked the question, "Who are you for real?" How would you respond?

Most people define themselves by their roles...I am a father, mother, sister, wife, etc; others by their accomplishments...I work for so and so, I have X amount of degrees, I am CEO of X company. However, those transient, ever-changing roles and accomplishments aren't who we are and often without warning God will unction us to shed the façade so that we can come to know our true selves.

God is very clear on who He is. In Exodus 3:13–14 this is how God defines Himself to Moses at the burning bush.

Then Moses said to God, "Indeed, *when* I come to the children of Israel and say to them, 'The God of your fathers has sent me to you,' and they say to me, 'What *is* His name?' what shall I say to them?" And God said to Moses, "I AM WHO I AM." And He said, "Thus you shall say to the children of Israel, 'I AM has sent me to you.'"

In Revelations 22:13, God declares of Himself, "I am the Alpha and the Omega, *the* Beginning and *the* End, the First and the Last." As if that wasn't enough, a loving God reveals to us through scripture more of Himself. The Word tells us that He is:

- El Shaddai (Lord God Almighty)
- Yahweh (Lord Jehovah)
- Jehovah Nissi (The Lord My Banner)
- Jehovah Rapha (The Lord that Heals)
- Again, God is very clear on who He is. Are you?

From a psychological perspective, Carl Rogers theorized that there is an Actual Self (who you really are) and an Ideal Self (who you think you should be). When you build your identity apart from Christ, you come to be what you were not intended to be. You come to believe that your roles define you and live as a human "doings" rather than human beings. I tell you the truth, it is only in Christ that you become the real you that God knew from the beginning. Through the process of surrender and specifically death of the flesh through your cross experience you come face to face with you; the real you that God refers to in Jeremiah 1:5, "Before I formed you in the womb I knew you; before you were born I sanctified you; I ordained you a prophet to the nations."

Getting to the real you takes work. I am a living witness. Many years ago, God had to isolate me and bring me to a place of brokenness for the real me to emerge. Then and only then did I come to the realization that I could lose everything and be something because of Christ. Now I am no longer fearful of walking away from a job, a role, a relationship. It's all for naught, unless it's for Christ. Therefore, it is in this space of surrender that I am becoming all that God imagined from the beginning. I am definitely a work in progress, but as I surrender more and more of myself to Him, I come to look more and more like His Son. His son died on a cross and so will I because surrender requires it.

FIVE

Surrender Paves the Way

"Follow Me"

Jesus extends the invitation to follow Him. It's up to us to accept.

Let's get something clear. To follow is to go after, move or travel behind. It's not to get ahead, or direct. The most challenging part of surrendering is the release of control. That's probably what makes it such an unpopular concept.

However, if you are going to succeed at following Christ, you will need to purpose in your heart to surrender all of you: mind, body, and spirit. Being born again takes a moment of faith, but becoming like

Christ is a lifelong process that requires one to follow Him every step of the way in obedience.

While Jesus lived on earth He had many followers. We know of twelve in particular. These twelve were personally invited by Jesus to follow Him and they did so without hesitation.

Here was Matthew's invitation: "As Jesus passed on from there, He saw a man named Matthew sitting at the tax office. And He said to him, "Follow Me." So he arose and followed Him" (Matthew 9:9). Here was Peter and Andrew's invitation: "And Jesus, walking by the Sea of Galilee, saw two brothers, Simon called Peter, and Andrew his brother, casting a net into the sea; for they were fishermen. Then He said to them, 'Follow Me, and I will make you fishers of men.' They immediately left their nets and followed Him" (Matthew 4:18–20). Here was the invitation extended to James and John: "Going on from there, He saw two other brothers, James *the son* of Zebedee, and John his brother, in the boat with Zebedee their father, mending their nets. He called them, and immediately they left the boat and their father, and followed Him" (Matthew 4:21–22). And though not part of the 12 here was my invitation: "Celeste, stop doing everything you're doing, go home and listen for further instructions". And immediately I left everything to follow Him.

Although scripture doesn't indicate such, I would imagine that Jesus had a conversation with each of the 12 before He spoke the phrase "follow me". I would imagine that He spoke of a higher call and a greater sense of fulfillment. I would imagine that each sensed His passion and wanted to be part of something greater. They were willing to leave it all because they believed that with Jesus they could do more, be more and change the world.

Of all the disciples perhaps Matthew risked the most. He had to leave a lucrative career to follow Jesus. Sure, Peter and the others could fall back on fishing, but Matthew's willingness to follow Jesus left Him without a backup plan. As we learn from Matthew, sometimes the decision to follow Christ requires difficult or painful choices. However, like Matthew, we must decide to leave behind those things that would keep us from following Christ.

Of course, many of us sing songs like "I Surrender All" and "Withholding Nothing." But do we really mean those words in our heart? When God calls you to His plan, are you willing to surrender it all? Talk is cheap and our words lack meaning if we are unwilling to back them up with action. God is calling you to more. God is calling you to His higher calling. Follow Him!

I AM NOT MY FLESH

While writing this chapter, I received a question by email from a woman named Sandy regarding her poor eating habits. She wrote, "I know what to do when it comes to eating right and I want to do it, but I don't. Why is that?"

Sandy asked the ultimate "follow me" question. She touched on the #1 hindrance to following Christ—disobedience. In fact, obedience is the foundation of our success in Christ. Sandy's flesh does as it pleases, even when she doesn't want it to because it has not been subjected to full submission and surrender to the Holy Spirit. The Apostle Paul experienced a similar dilemma and offers hope for change in the book of Romans, chapter 7 where he makes a distinction between the true (spiritual) self and the sinful (fleshly) self. Just as India Arie sings, "I am not my hair," you should be saying, "I am not my flesh." The flesh, as used here, is not referring to the physical body, but to an attitude; a heart posture that is rebellious against God and righteousness. The flesh does what it wants to do, when it wants to do it, when left unchecked by the Spirit. But when you allow the Spirit to sanctify the flesh, you prosper and you win.

It's a fact that we cannot be well and whole apart from God. Sheer willpower will not produce the results we want. We are sold as a slave to sin, therefore just wanting or willing something to be different won't make it so. Don't believe me? How many times have you willed yourself to stop consuming sugar to only go back to it time and time again? Or how many times have you said I am going to control my tongue only to find yourself in a conversation you know is not godly. For that reason Paul wrote, "For what I am doing, I do not understand. For what I will to do, that I do not practice; but what I hate, that I do" (Romans 7:15).

This double-mindedness reflects the imbalance of power between our willpower and the power of the flesh. You can't conquer the flesh on your own; through sheer willpower. Only God can change you and cause you to win in areas of your life that you have failed in time and time again.

Accordingly, you must recognize that although you are in Christ and aware of sin, the flesh part of you still has real estate in your heart. Only through the sanctifying power of the Holy Spirit can you change beliefs, thoughts and actions. Again, just because you want to do something doesn't mean you will do it. Indeed, desire is the beginning of change, but it doesn't guarantee it. Change only happens when you change your mind. And a changed mind produces changed actions through supernatural empowerment from God. Until you get that, you will mess up over and over again.

However, before you go wallowing in self-pity or are overtaken with feelings of condemnation understand the truth: when you are in Christ you are a new creation. Therefore, when you go about doing what you don't want to do put the blame where it belongs, on the sin. Paul confirms this in Romans 7:20, "Now if I do what I will not *to do,* it is no longer

I who do it, but sin that dwells in me." So if it is the sin that does it, then sin of any kind that resides on the inside of you must be eliminated through repentance.

If you truly desire to follow Christ and not live in bondage to sin, start each day with repentance. Through repentance, you allow God to wash you clean and renew your mind to what is right. I hope you truly understand that following Christ is not about condemnation, but about partnership with Him to fulfill your life's call. You can do it! You can overcome the power to sin through Christ because you can do all things through Him as He strengthens you.

Lastly, in addition to obedience, if you are to succeed at following Christ you will have to exercise the following: discretion, discernment, and the pursuit of divine connections.

DISCRETION

Discretion is wisely choosing to do what is right. It's also knowing when to speak and when to keep silent. Jesus' directive to "Follow Me" is not merely the following of His direction, but also the following of His example. Jesus was the master of discretion; He always chose to do what was right. He also knew when to speak and when to bridle His tongue.

For example, a woman, caught in the act of adultery, was brought before Jesus (John 8:1–11). The rulers of that day, had hoped to trick Jesus into disobeying the law of Moses, and thus put Him in a precarious situation. As was the custom, the adulterous woman should have been stoned. However, Jesus in a manner typical of Him did what was unexpected. After a period of silence, then writing in the dust, He invited the accuser that was without sin to cast the first stone. There was not one.

There is much to be learned from Jesus' care of this woman on that day and how His discretion blessed her and others that witnessed His love. One, He didn't jump to judgment. When we follow Jesus' guide to be discreet, we do the same. We demonstrate His love by covering the other person and not rushing to judgment. We are reminded in scripture that love believes the best of every person no matter the situation. In *Marriage Undercover*, author Bob Meisner relays his reaction to his wife's disclosure that she had had an affair. His first instinct was to uncover her shame; to make her hurt as much as she had hurt him. However, after speaking with another godly leader he chose to use discretion and to cover her sin.

You may be experiencing a similar hurt; someone may have hurt you deeply and caused you great pain, but instead of judging and lashing out, follow Jesus' example to be discreet. My friend, love is discreet; it covers a multitude of sins and when your heart has been transformed by God's love you will yourself to be quiet about another's sin. Indeed, a heart that forgives does so because he knows how much he has been forgiven.

A second lesson on discretion to be learned from this story is that discretion should be followed even when it is unpopular or has the potential to put us in an unfavorable light. So often we abandon discretion in an effort to please men. Jesus certainly could have followed the crowd, accused this woman outright and punished her by stoning. However, He chose the less traveled path of forgiveness and understanding. He chose to see beyond the woman's behavior and love her anyway. Isn't that what He does for us? Then how much more should we do the same?

I can recall a time when I was working with a government official assisting her with providing community service to the residents in her county. She was later accused of a crime and removed from office. Just a day after her arrest a woman said to me, "I heard about your friend" and the way she said *friend* indicated that she expected me to betray this woman to save face. I was double-minded on this issue. One part of me wanted to protect and cover this woman who had become my friend; however, the other part wanted to be absolved of any affiliation with her to protect my own reputation—you know the saying, "birds of a feather flock together". Nonetheless, I chose discretion; I chose to follow Jesus' example and to do what was right. You best believe this stance didn't increase my popularity in this conversation or others that followed, but to be in right standing with God is more important to me than pleasing man. Additionally, it wasn't my place to say anything about my friend because I didn't have the full story. The Word tells us in Psalm 34:13 to keep our tongues from evil. Sometimes we talk out of turn without knowing the full story and that is evil. In Proverbs 6:16–17a it is written, "These six *things* the Lord hates, Yes, seven *are* an abomination to Him: a proud look, a lying tongue." When we speak of things that we don't know much about, this is an abomination to God and He is greatly displeased. Again, Jesus demonstrated to us how important discretion is in times like these even when we think we have the full story as it appeared that Jesus did. She was caught in the very act of adultery; enough said right? Wrong. It is not for us to be the judge and jury of another or to behave in an unloving manner. It is for us to love one another and to use discretion.

Lastly, a lack of discretion can be detrimental not only to others, but to ourselves. You may recall the story of Moses who prematurely jumped into the role of savior for his people. One day as he observed the plight of his people he witnessed the mistreatment of a Hebrew slave by one of the Egyptian task masters. He was livid and killed the overseer. The next day he attempted to break up a fight between two Hebrew men. He was shocked to find out that they knew of his crime. He fled Egypt to not be seen again for 40 years. Here's the issue. It wasn't that Moses had not been called to save his people from slavery, but that his pride blinded him from discretion. Whenever we are caught up in pride, we make hasty decisions like sharing with another person something God desires for us to keep to ourselves. Proverbs 4:14–15 reads, "Do not enter the path of the wicked, and do not walk in the way of evil. Avoid it, do not travel on it; turn away from it and pass on." If we are being prideful, we are walking the same road as the wicked. It is okay to boast in the Lord, but bragging about His goodness to make you look better is wrong and shows a lack of discretion.

DISCERNMENT

To have discernment is to know the difference between good and bad, right and wrong. It also includes the ability to grasp and comprehend what is obscure. Proverbs 14:12 tells us that, "There is a way *that seems* right to a man, but its end *is* the way of death."

If you are a follower of Christ you have the ability to discern. The gift of the Holy Spirit makes this possible. One of my favorite scriptures comes from Jeremiah 33:3 which reads, "Call to Me, and I will answer you, and show you great and mighty things, which you do not know." I pray this prayer in all sorts of situations, but I find it especially effective when I am speaking with someone who needs my advice. I take advice-giving seriously and look to the Lord for the words of encouragement that will set the person free. So while they are speaking I pray and ask God to show me the "fenced-in" things; to give me discernment and revelation that can only come from Him. And He answers. By the time the conversation has ended, God has done an amazing work through the power of discernment.

I can recall a time in my life that I needed discernment in a major way. It was when I desired to be married. Although I wasn't sure to whom, or even if marriage was part of God's plan for me, I still strongly desired a mate. However, after making a mess of things and dating all the wrong guys, I decided to surrender my singleness to the Lord. This was at the urging of P.B. "Bunny" Wilson, the author of *Knight in Shining Armor*. No, she didn't personally ask me to stop dating, but the contract at the front of her book suggested that I not date for 6 months and I complied.

Mind you, this wasn't an easy decision. I had bought into the idea that a good man was hard to find and the others were either gay and/or in jail. So, in my opinion, complying with the request to wait 6 months was a waste of valuable time! However, I had made such a mess of things that I couldn't imagine that God could do worse. In fact, desperation had caused me to take some wrong turns and when desperation is present, discernment is not.

So I signed the contract and went about living life as a satisfied single. I soon discovered that there was much that God had for me to do as a single and contentment became real. In fact, I became so engrossed in living out God's call for me as a single that when Mr. Right walked up, I barely noticed him.

It was at a wedding. My friend from college was marrying her Boaz and I was a bridesmaid. Unbeknownst to me, the best man and brother to the groom, was my future husband. God had set it all up, nearly six months to the day of my signing that contract.

Again I wasn't looking for Andel; he found me. In fact, the Holy Spirit had to nudge me to pay attention. At the reception while we both wrapped our gifts to the couple (yes, we were both a little disorganized and waited to the 11th hour to wrap gifts) we discovered we had the same wedding cards; his purchased in Maryland and mine in Pennsylvania. The moment that discovery was made the Holy Spirit whispered, "pay attention." He didn't have to suggest that twice. We sat on a bench talking for most of the reception, were engaged 5 months later, and have been happily married ever since.

When Jesus says follow me, He does so knowing that He has good plans for you. He asked me to stop dating. Doing so made my path straight and caused me to prosper. Had I decided to continue on the path that *seemed* right to me, who knows where I would be today?

If you desire to be a victor each and every day, pray, then ask God for discernment and wisdom. As we are reminded in 1 Peter 5:8, "Be sober, be vigilant; because your adversary the devil walks about like a roaring lion, seeking whom he may devour."

The enemy is cunning and he will send distractors and distractions to confuse you, but with God ever present, you will make the right decisions and you will be victorious.

Speaking of hasty decisions and how this implies a lack of discernment, I can't tell you how many times God has spoken a word to me and I've run ahead to make it happen. But take it from me, slow down; God's timing is perfect and we need His direction to succeed. The Word tells us in Proverbs 19:2, "Desire without knowledge is not good—how much more will hasty feet miss the way!"

Some years ago, my spiritual mentor said to me these words, "It's time—get your passport." In haste, I ran out the next week to get my passport. Imagine my chagrin when two years later I hadn't traveled farther than Canada. The best advice I can offer you is that when God speaks a word listen, thank Him, pray, and then wait for further instructions. God always speaks in the present and we are reminded that one day is as a thousand years to God. So again, slow down and be patient. God can be trusted.

Remember, not every good opportunity is a God opportunity. In today's society, we are busy for the sake of being busy; we are busy without being productive. God is a God of purpose. When God sends you an opportunity, He does so with eternity in mind. And what I love about God is that His opportunities are accompanied by grace. I've often heard, "I don't know how you do all that you are doing." I am surprised by that comment because I don't feel like I am doing much. Of course, when I think about the things I am doing I understand their comment, but truthfully with grace on my side I often feel I am at rest. That's what God's grace does—makes you feel as if you aren't working at all.

If you are not experiencing God's rest in your endeavors, if you are sick, tired, and overwhelmed it's time to take stock of what you are doing. When you take opportunities that are not from Him—often in an effort to fill a void that can only be filled by God—you become overwhelmed and over-extended. Being over-obligated is a trick of the enemy to keep you bound and unproductive. His job is to bring death and being over-obligated is death. But Christ came that you might have life and more abundantly. Abundant life comes when you are in the downtown will of God. Discernment allows you to be there.

I can recall both the excitement and fear I felt in 2009 when God called me to leave all that I was doing to follow Him to an unknown place. I would like to say that I followed this plan perfectly, but that would be a lie. At the end of that year, I received an unexpected call from the ministry leader who had taken over the position I had released. Innocently enough she asked if I would be willing to do the administrative tasks of the ministry. I readily accepted. However, before the call ended the Holy Spirit warned me that I had made the wrong decision. I chose to ignore Him. Needless to say, I had no peace for the rest of the day and the next morning I phoned the ministry leader to tell her I had to decline her offer. I felt terrible going back on my word and my pride was hurt, but staying in a place where God had instructed me to leave would have been much more detrimental. Even now, I am thanking Him for His grace and the ability to discern what is right and be obedient to His will and plan.

DIVINE CONNECTIONS

It is said that success comes by who you know and not what you know. I completely agree if the "Who" is referring to God. He is the Who we need to know. He will direct you to the right people, at the right time if you would just follow Him.

I, for one, find this comforting. As an introvert, I am not designed to pursue people with the intensity and ferocity of my extroverted counterparts. In fact, I find networking meetings down right painful. If you feel the same way, I have good news for you. Pursue God and He will pave the way for you. He will open doors that can't be closed and allow your gift to make room for you and bring you before great men. Aren't you glad we serve a God of divine connections?

Connections are hugely important to God. His Word tells us that where two or three are gathered together in His name there He will be in the midst. In Psalm 133, David reminds us of how good and pleasant it is for brothers to dwell in unity. If you are uncomfortable with the idea of connecting or even needing others to survive and succeed, surrender that fear to God. You will not complete your kingdom assignment without other people. In fact, every instance in the Bible where man advanced it was with the aid or help of something or someone. So if you are willing, God has the plan to divinely connect you with the right people.

There is a story in the Bible that demonstrates this perfectly. In Genesis 24, Abraham desired to find a wife for his son Isaac. He commanded his servant to go to the land of his forefathers to find Isaac a wife. The servant doubted his ability to be successful in this endeavor so he asked for God's favor and a divine connection. He specifically prayed that the young woman that was for Isaac would offer him water and then water for his camels.

On the other side of that prayer, and unbeknownst to the servant, God had sent an angel beforehand to prepare the way. And only as God can do it, before the servant had finished praying the young woman Rebecca approached to offer him and the camels water. In just a matter of minutes, God had answered the servant's prayer! The servant didn't have to conduct interviews or randomly pick a woman he thought might be suitable. No, he instead decided to follow God and it worked out in his favor.

When I think of the vastness of God's vision for my life and the steps that need to be taken to get there, I can get overwhelmed. I don't know where to start or who to ask for help, but God does. So as I continue this journey I am constantly praying to God for the right connections, that my name be dropped in unusual places, and that my gift would make room for me and bring me before great and mighty men.

During the course of my writing this book, I decided to boot fear out the door, and to boldly declare "yes" to divine expansion, divine connections, divine provision, and divine favor. The impossible is made possible when we say yes. In fact, when we do so a shift occurs that allows what is already done in heaven to be manifested on earth. When you say yes you give God permission to show up and show out in your life.

As God begins to expand and enlarge your territory don't simply think that advancement only comes from your connections to powerful people or those of high influence in our society. Be open to God using most anyone or anything to make His plan manifest. Surrender to God's divine connections even when you think the person has no ability to advance God's kingdom assignment in your life. Who would have thought that a boy with a packed lunch would be instrumental in the miracle that Jesus performed when He fed the five thousand? Who would have thought that a talking donkey could keep a man from taking the wrong path and being struck down by God for disobedience? Who would have thought that a baby born and raised on the wrong side of the tracks would become the savior of the world? Don't underestimate any of God's creations. He will use whom He pleases, when He pleases to advance you in His kingdom assignment and when it is all said and done He will get all the glory.

GOD'S PROMISES COME WITH CONDITIONS

God's promises are sure and they will come to pass. The Word tells us so. We read in Joshua 21:45, "Not a word failed of any good thing which the Lord had spoken to the house of Israel. All came to pass."

However, if your life is anything like mine, somewhere in your journey you've experienced some unanswered promises. I'm not talking about things you *thought* you heard the Lord say, or things you made up to be true because you wanted them so badly. No; I am talking about promises you *knew* the Lord had promised. Promises you were willing to look foolish for, that you shared with others and invited them to witness God move in an amazing way in your life. That same promise that later devastated your faith as it was delayed and then died.

In the writing of this book, my friend and her husband experienced this very thing. The house they were waiting on, the house God had promised was theirs, sold. How could that be? Had God reneged on His promise? Like them I, too, had experienced the devastation of not having a promise fulfilled. So as my friend and her husband grieved the loss of their beloved home, I sought the Lord for answers and they did too and what we learned is that God hadn't reneged on His promise; He had planned to do just as He said, but the fulfillment of that plan came with conditions.

Deuteronomy 28 reads, "Now it shall come to pass, if you diligently obey the voice of the Lord your God, to observe carefully all His commandments which I command you today, that the Lord your God will set you high above all nations of the earth. And all these blessings shall come upon you and overtake you, because you obey the voice of the Lord your God." What a glorious promise. However, we can misinterpret this scripture if we miss the "if" seven words into this verse. It's not enough to embrace the phrase "now it shall come to pass" and run with the promise of being overtaken by the blessings if we are unwilling to pursue with the same passion the condition that God has attached to this promise. And that condition is obedience.

In other words, if we are going to see a mighty move of God in our life and be privy to the glorious promises He has laid out before us we have to do our part. I am not preaching a works mentality for indeed when we are caught up in works for the sake of works we are pushing our agenda and not His. However, the Word tells us that faith without works is dead and when we believe that to be true, we willingly collaborate with God to bring about His will here on earth as it is already done in heaven. Again if we are going to see the manifestation of what God said He would do, we have to do our part; we have to follow Him and allow surrender to pave the way.

It takes a lot of humility and courage to go back and learn from those times we have missed God. But do it. As you surrender to the truth, you pave the way to God's bigger and His greater. No matter what missteps you've taken, you have not aborted God's plan for you. He still plans to bring you to His expected end, your best days are still in front of you, and eyes have not seen nor ears heard what God has in store for you!

SIX

Surrender Resurrects

"Whoever loses his life for me will find it."

By way of definition, an oxymoron is a combination of contradictory words that most think shouldn't be linked together. God's word is full of oxymorons and the scripture that reads, "whoever loses his life for me will find it" is no exception. In fact, whenever Jesus spoke one was sure to hear some seemingly contradictory phrase leave His lips.

You may be wondering *can losing my life for God really empower me to find it*? Yes! Again we have no better example than in our Lord and Savior Jesus

Christ and no chapter on resurrection would be complete without talking about The Resurrection.

Thankfully, Jesus is not merely a heavenly ruler that requires of us of what He has no knowledge. No; when Jesus speaks of losing your life to find it or gain from it, He does so from experience. When the time was right, He was released to earthly ministry. When the time was right, He was empowered to perform many miracles. And when the time was right, He surrendered His life to death. But that is not how the story ends. For when the time was right, Jesus was resurrected and ascended back to His Father, and in the end—when the time is right—every knee will bow and every tongue shall confess that Jesus is Lord. Now that's how you lose to gain!

The Word tells us, "Now a man was sick, Lazarus of Bethany." You probably know the story. In a nutshell, word is sent to Jesus, He tarries, and Lazarus dies. Upon His arrival to Bethany, He was interrogated by the grieving Martha whose negative posture caused Him to weep. She thought the story had ended, but, indeed, she had come face-to-face with the Resurrection and her life would forever be changed. With just 3 words, "Lazarus come forth!" he who was dead came forth and lived and with those same 3 words Martha's life was transformed. In her *loss* she *gained* a greater understanding of who Jesus is. That's exactly what we gain when we lose too. In fact, every time we lose our lives for His, we gain more and more of Him.

LINE UP WITH GOD'S INTENTIONS BY WATCHING YOUR WORDS

Like Martha, what dead situation are you facing? How are you speaking during your wait? Don't be like Martha who lost all hope. Believe like Abraham, choosing faith rather than doubt, knowing that God can and will do just as He promised.

If it is God's intention to resurrect your dead situation, then your words have to line up with His plan. Before God sent Jesus to this earth the world was in a dead situation. In the midst of what seemed hopeless, God was planning the ultimate resurrection.

The angel Gabriel was sent by God to a town in Galilee to a virgin that was engaged to a man named

Joseph. Her name was Mary and she had found favor
in the sight of God. Gabriel proclaimed,

> "Rejoice, highly favored *one,* the Lord *is* with
> you; blessed *are* you among women! Do not
> be afraid, Mary, for you have found favor with
> God. And behold, you will conceive in your
> womb and bring forth a Son, and shall call
> His name JESUS. He will be great, and will
> be called the Son of the Highest; and the Lord
> God will give Him the throne of His father
> David. And He will reign over the house of
> Jacob forever, and of His kingdom there will
> be no end" (Luke 1:28b, 30–33).

What an awesome word and promise from God
to Mary. Through her, God was planning to reconcile
man back to Him. However, the way Mary responded
to this plan was crucial. Indeed, she could have
responded any number of ways, but she responded
correctly. She simply asked how this could be so as she
had never been with a man. When Gabriel explained
how the process would take place, Mary didn't argue
with him; she simply affirmed her faith in God's plan

with these words, "Behold the maidservant of the Lord! Let it be to me according to your word." And it was done.

When God shows up with unbelievable news for you, like Mary will you believe? Will God be able to say about you, "blessed is (s)he who believed what was spoken to him/her." If you are going to move from here to there, from natural to supernatural, what you say regarding your situation is crucial. I don't care what it looks like right now, when God makes you a promise it's always "yes and amen" and He is able to do just as He said.

Zachariah, the father of John the Baptist, wasn't so convinced of God's power to do the impossible and it cost him. Six months prior to Mary's Immaculate Conception, Zachariah, a priest, was visited by an angel from the Lord. The bible says that Zachariah and his wife Elizabeth were righteous in the sight of the Lord and walked blameless in all His commandments, but they were without child for Elizabeth was barren. The angel said to him, "Do not be afraid, Zachariah, for your prayer is heard; and your wife Elizabeth will bear you a son, and you shall call his name John"

(Luke 1:13). He goes on to say that the child will be great in the sight of the Lord and he will be filled with the Holy Spirit. He will also turn the hearts of the children of Israel back to God. Zachariah's response to this proclamation came with consequences. He immediately questioned the angel's statement by suggesting his wife was too old to conceive. For his unbelief he is rendered mute until the birth of his child.

You might ask, why was Mary allowed to question the angel and Zachariah was not. I believe it comes down to the intent of the heart. Mary's response to the angel wasn't rooted in a lack of faith but a curiosity about how she a virgin could become pregnant. On the other hand, Zachariah didn't believe what the angel had spoken and wanted God to prove to him that it could be done.

If you want God to resurrect a dead situation in your life, you will have to watch your words. He has proven Himself faithful—he has opened doors for you, healed your body, and made a way out of no one. God is a God of consistency. He is the same yesterday, today and forever (Hebrews 13:8). If he showed you yesterday what He is capable of, what makes you think that tomorrow will be any different? He can do the impossible and resurrect the very thing you think has died.

Therefore, exercise your faith and grab hold of His Word to you in this season. He is about to do a new thing and take you where you haven't been. He is going to bless you beyond your wildest dreams if you will just believe.

RESURRECTION REQUIRES BROKENNESS

This probably won't be the most popular section of the book but it is necessary. The truth of the matter is that resurrection does not come without brokenness. Oftentimes we have to go back in order to move forward. My friend Crystal Prater said, "When you come to the end of yourself, you find yourself." In other words, where you end, God begins.

Brian Hardin, the founder of the Daily Audio Bible has a phenomenal testimony of how God used brokenness to resurrect his true self. Brian grew up a preacher's kid and vowed to never be a minister;

instead, music was his thing. He met with some success in the music industry but in the end music failed him and he found himself bankrupt, both financially and emotionally.

With all that had happened he had come to the end of himself. Despondent and broken he prayed this prayer to our risen Savior, "Jesus I'm done with the crap. I'm finished. If you want me to go to Des Moines and make hamburgers for a living, I'll pack up our stuff tomorrow and leave. I'm fine with that." That simple, might I add raggedy, surrender prayer turned his life around. From his place of brokenness God's plan began to unfold. First, He instructed him to create a podcast of himself reading the bible. He had no idea what a podcast was, but He knew God was calling him to this, so he did his homework. Eventually, he recorded his first podcast and the rest is history. Today more than 64 million people have downloaded his podcast. He is reaching the world and advancing the kingdom because he allowed God to resurrect his life story from his place of brokenness.

Getting to the end of yourself is no small feat; it takes a leap of faith. But your yes is going to open doors for you. Your complete surrender is releasing you to do exceedingly above all you can ask or think. Don't give up or give in; this is your time of expectancy. Those dreams that God has planted inside you are about to be realized. In your spiritual womb, God has planted the seed of His anointing and you are now pregnant with your destiny. A praise should be on your lips and the air should be ripe with expectation because He is about to do a new thing in you and through you. God is about to do what He has promised and no devil in hell can stop Him. God has all authority and He will resurrect your dead situation in His time and after you have been broken.

CLUTTER WILL BLOCK A RESURRECTION

In the process of writing this book, I specifically asked God to resurrect my speaking career. Prior to coming home in 2010, I was speaking at least 4–6 times per month. Fast forward 5 years and it felt as if I was speaking 4–6 times per year! But I knew that things were turning around for me. So I prayed.

"Lord you said in your Word to seek ye first the kingdom and all these things will be added. So what is the kingdom?" His instructions to me were to pray, study, and declutter. The first two made perfect sense. But declutter?! What does clutter have to do with anything? As I learned from my studies, clutter has a lot to do with my not moving forward.

Of course, I know nothing can happen before God's ordered time; however, I also know that I can delay my forward movement if I'm not in position to receive. So the day I heard God say declutter, I did a thorough examination of my home. I was determined to throw or give away the things I didn't need. Needless to say, it was a big job. How had I become so cluttered? Mine wasn't a messy clutter as most things had a nice little nook or cute storage bin to hang out in. What I had before me were years of things I couldn't part with. All of the *one-day-I-might-need* items, that would probably never have a day. So in obedience I started purging. I wasn't willing to allow my excess to hinder my forward movement or the resurrection I so deeply desired.

If you have clutter this section is for you. First, let's examine what the clutter is all about. We all have some clutter but excessive clutter is the problem; it holds one back from making progress. In fact, clutter represents postponed decisions and an inability to move forward. Clutter also represents stagnation and procrastination. Indeed, nothing new flows into your life until you make room for it. And as I looked around my house, I realized that the clutter was keeping me from moving forward in the new things that God had for me.

Second, what keeps us holding on is fear. We fear that if we let go, those things will never be replaced. Not so. God is a God of abundance and has greater for each of us but the environment has to be conducive for His greater to flow. God is a God of order. I Corinthians 14:33a reads, "For God is not *the author* of confusion but of peace." Some other translations say that He is not the God of disorder. If that be true, how can His plans flourish in an environment of clutter and chaos?

So let me encourage you today to examine your clutter and purge any and every thing that you don't need. It won't be easy; you may even cry. But if you want God's abundance to flow through your life with freedom and ease you must remove those things that hinder Him from doing so.

RESURRECTION CAN OCCUR SUDDENLY

Brokenness not only brings about resurrection, but it also produces obedience. Obedience is no cakewalk. What must Abraham have experienced when he was asked to sacrifice his son? "Take your son, your only son, Isaac, whom you love, and go to the region of Moriah. Sacrifice him there as a burnt offering" (Genesis 22:2a). And not only did Abraham hear the word but he was a doer. He proceeded to make plans to sacrifice his son! Thankfully God had a ram in the bush. However, it's important to understand how Abraham was able to be obedient in a literal life or death situation. He was able to pass this particular test because he had passed many others prior. Although this was the most severe of them all, Abraham's prior acts of obedience had allowed him to learn that God could be trusted.

You won't ever get to what is big if you keep failing at what is little. The word tells us that if we faint in the day of adversity our strength is small. The way to build your strength is by trusting God and being obedient to His commands. In fact, every time we say "no" or "yes" with conditions we hinder God from moving in a mighty way in our lives and lose the opportunity to build our faith. However, Abraham seized every moment and opportunity to let God be God. Although God provided a ram in the bush, Abraham had no prior knowledge that that would be his fate. In his heart Isaac was already dead and yet he would trust God.

I've had similar experiences. Just when it appeared that a situation was completely dead, the Lord resurrects. For example, my church declared 2015 to be the year of restoration. One thing I wanted restored was my speaking platform. Specifically, that doors would open for me to speak internationally. Many years ago God had pronounced me an "International Healing Ministry." He did so at a time when I was far from any type of healing ministry—let alone international. However, when I heard God say these things about me in my spirit and they were confirmed by a woman I trusted in ministry, I ran out to get my passport. There is something to be said about zeal. Nonetheless, for four years I had nothing to show for my faith except two stamps, both from the Bahamas for pleasure trips. Funny. However, when God makes a promise He keeps it.

So in the spring of 2015, I was invited to speak at Temple of Praise International Church in Beltsville, MD. It was truly a divine connection. An associate pastor for that church had heard me speak at the Bible Study I taught for my home church. In turn, he invited to me speak at two of his services. When I arrived that Wednesday night, I was immediately overwhelmed by the sovereignty of God. On both sides of the sanctuary were rows of flags from every country imaginable. I was reminded in that moment that God had not forgotten that I was an international healing ministry. I shared with the church what God revealed to me before rising to speak and they agreed that God had released me for international ministry from their pulpit. As the old song goes, "Ain't that a wonder about Jesus." In just a matter of seconds God

had resurrected a dream long forgotten and to seal
the deal the next day I received the following email:

> Thank God for the good work that you are
> doing for him, which I have just seen on
> your website; that is why I have decided to
> contact you to share ideas of our ministry
> work together. I am the senior pastor of Word
> of Life Harvest Church in Eldoret, Kenya
> and a National overseer. I would also like to
> share with you about our coming Leadership
> Conference in Kenya. I am requesting you to
> come and speak to our Leaders' conference
> early next year if God leads you. Your
> experience in the ministry work will help
> our Leaders; most of our Leaders need to be
> empowered and equipped with the word of
> God. Let me hear from you if God is leading
> you to come and empower our Leaders so that
> we can send to you our conference schedule.
> Let me hear your thoughts. In Christ's service
> and Love, Bishop Chris and Tabitha

Only God can orchestrate events in such a way. That Sunday when I read this letter to Temple of Praise they rejoiced with me for what God had done. And not only that, they pledged to pay my airfare to Kenya! Not only does God give a vision, He also gives provision. All He requires is a "yes" and full surrender of our lives to Him.

SEE IT BEFORE YOU SEE IT

While in the process of writing this book, I had an enlightening conversation with my friend Alita Gaskill. Although she was in a challenging season of her life, she refused to believe that her circumstances defined her; she was determined to believe God no matter what. Accordingly, as we were in conversation, she made a powerful declaration that won't let me loose. She said that in order to witness the manifestation of God's promises, "you have to see it before you see it."

Did you hear that? You have to see it before you see it. The Word tells us in Hebrews 11:1, "Now faith is the substance of things hoped for, the evidence of things not seen" and according to Romans 4:17 we have to "call those things which are not, as if they are so". In other words, you have to see it before you see it.

By nature I am a pessimist. I've worked hard to rise above this personality weakness and see my circumstances through the eyes of faith. In fact, God has blessed me so much in this area that most people who know me now would not characterize me as a pessimist. Nonetheless seeing something before I see something is truly a challenge for my melancholy, the "glass is half empty" personality. But when God wrote in his word that He is moved by faith and without faith it is impossible to please Him, He was talking to everyone—even the pessimist. Therefore, in order to witness resurrection in your life you must show God your faith.

Two tools that have helped me to see a thing before it is evident in my life are visualization and affirmation. Visualization is the process of creating a mind picture of something that you would like to see happen in your life. Affirmations, on the other hand, are verbal confirmation of what you can see. Once I can see it, I can say it.

If you are in need of a resurrection in your life, let me encourage you that God can do it. He is not like man that He would lie. If he said it would be done, it's already done. In fact, He holds His word above His name and when He decrees a thing you best believe it will come to pass. Just keep the faith.

There was a time in my life that I was in need of a serious resurrection. It was in 2014. God had told me that my church would do *The 40-Day Surrender Fast*. I had no idea how to make that happen, so I waited on the Lord. Going back a little, in April of 2013, a member of my church's New Year's Fasting Committee phoned me to say that they were considering my book for their New Year's time of fasting. Needless to say I was ecstatic. Four or five months passed before I heard from them again, but nonetheless they were still strongly considering the book. By that December my dreams were crushed; our Pastor had not approved my book as the fast for the New Year. I phoned my sister, who at the time was my accountability partner. I can remember it like it was yesterday. I shared with her the decision and she didn't flinch. She said with conviction, "God said First Baptist Church of Glenarden will do the fast; therefore they will." And with that I started seeing it before I would see it. I started speaking it before it was manifest.

True story. I would sit in church and while the pastor was preaching I would visualize myself in the pulpit sharing with the congregation. I also printed a picture of my pastor in our pulpit and I would see myself there instead. After a while, the image was so ingrained in my psyche that I knew without a shadow of a doubt it would come to pass. When I would speak with my prayer partner or a few select friends I would tell them that I couldn't wait until the church did the book. I was that confident.

Well my faith paid off. Out of the blue in April 2014 I received a call from my pastor that he was starting a series in the Bible Study on fasting and that he was going to mention my book. I was beyond thrilled. He wasn't going to do it, but a mention was good enough for me. But much to my surprise, that evening at Bible Study not only did the pastor mention the book, he announced that the church would be doing the fast! God's word had come to pass. My faith had made the seemingly impossible, possible and God had resurrected my dream. All because I was able to see it before I could see it.

SEVEN

Surrender Advances

*"For what profit is it to a man if he gains
the whole world, and loses his own soul?"*

What would gaining the world profit you? Zero, zip, zilch, nada. To gain the world and to lose your soul is no profit at all. In fact, true success is only achieved through obedience to God's plan for your life. Let it be known, God's position is clear—it is only what we do for Christ that will last; all the rest is temporary and has no significance in the span of eternity. Proverbs 19:21 reads, "many plans are in a man's mind, but it is the Lord's purpose for him that will stand."

Free-Online Dictionary defines success as the achievement of something desired, planned, or attempted. This broad definition allows success to be both personal and subjective. It appreciates each person's unique space in the world acknowledging that not everyone was called to be a doctor or a lawyer. Each person has, however, been called by God for a specific, unique assignment. Some will be homemakers while others high-powered, corporate executives. In God's economy, one isn't more valuable than the other.

Unfortunately, our society has narrowed its view of success, suggesting that it is merely the attainment of power, money, and status. According to this worldview, greatness is obtained via fame and fortune and only an elite few ever "make it." Even the church has adopted a secular understanding of success, equating fame with greatness and money with faith. Accordingly, in some churches leadership positions are reserved almost exclusively for those congregants with significant financial standing or clout in the community. Those deemed "unsuccessful" are ignored and considered unworthy to lead God's people.

In other instances, the wildly popular "prosperity gospel" has poisoned the minds of the saints. This "name it and claim it" and "blab it and grab it" theology suggests that financial wealth is God's plan for every Christian, but it neglects to take into account that God's plan for each individual is not simply a matter of dollars and cents. He could care less about making you rich if that means that you will turn your back on Him. Yes, God is about prosperity, but in a holistic fashion. He desires that you prosper in all things and be in health, just as your soul prospers (3 John 1:2). If monetary gain is part of His plan for your life—great. However, I pray your desire for wealth is not simply to feed your hedonistic desires, but for the purpose of serving others and drawing souls to the kingdom.

Sadly, this overemphasis on prospering in the material de-emphasizes what is most important— prospering in the ways of God. If you believe that success stems from obeying God and doing what He has called you to do, you will find contentment and fulfillment. But if worldly success is your standard, your way will be wrought with exhaustion, disappointment, and frustration. Therefore, it is imperative that you define success on God's terms, not the world's, that you learn how surrendering to God's will and plan truly advances.

SUCCEEDING GOD'S WAY

Pastor Tony Evans of the Urban Alternative has stated that if you are prospering and doing well in activities that are not ordained by God, you are a successful failure. One is only truly successful when one operates according to God's plan for his/her life. God's position is clear—it is only what we do for Christ that will last (see 2 Corinthians 5:10; 1 Corinthians 3:11–15); all the rest is temporary and has no significance in the span of eternity. Proverbs 19:21 reads, "many plans are in a man's mind, but it is the Lord's purpose for him that will stand."

The individual who succeeds God's way is productive, creative, and fruitful. He is not simply busying himself with useless tasks to "look" successful, but is purposeful in his dealings. He cuts out those activities that are not profitable to the kingdom so that he doesn't go through life at such a frantic pace.

Busyness is a tool of the enemy. He strives to convince us that we can do it all: family, career, social and community obligations. He works to create a mindset of excess, that quantity is better than quality and that doing trumps being. In time, we grow to believe our sense of worth is directly tied to how much we do and that respect and admiration is a result of our doing. This is simply not true. It is a lie from the pit that when believed keeps us distracted, unfocused and unproductive.

In a culture that emphases the importance of "doing," it's a challenge to stay focused and not succumb to the pressure. This has been a societal problem for centuries. The people inquired of Jesus, "What are we to do to carry out what God requires?" (John 6:28). Indeed they expected Jesus to suggest acts of service: healing the sick, preaching the gospel, or building new synagogues. But Jesus replied, "This is the work of God, that you believe in Him whom He sent" (John 6:29). Simply put we won't achieve until we believe! In other words, all of our efforts will be rendered null and void if we do not believe in Jesus. Likewise, when we believe in Him we make every effort to live productive, purposeful lives.

So what's the difference between busyness and godly productiveness? The fruit. Busyness is burdensome, frustrating, and draining. When people are busy, they aren't enjoyable and others aren't seeking their company. They complain, whine, and blame everyone else for their plight. They have health problems—hypertension, joint pain, gastrointestinal illnesses, migraines and other conditions—with no known medical explanation. In fact, when busyness has run its course the recipient is left with nothing but a nice dose of burnout.

Godly productiveness on the other hand brings joy, peace, and a sense of accomplishment. This person is a joy to be around and the love of God radiates from them like a beacon of light and hope. Others seek their company and want to emulate them because they emulate Christ.

Unfortunately, it appears that we are especially susceptible to the disease of busyness in the church.

Some churches expect ministry involvement to have no limits. Members are discouraged, either overtly or covertly, from having a life outside of the church and are expected to be available both day and night. It is not wise to act in this way. In fact the scripture says, "This wisdom does not descend from above, but *is* earthly, sensual, demonic" (James 3:15). God requires us to do His will which includes prioritizing our responsibilities. We are not to neglect the needs of our family, our health, and private time with God for the church.

Yet so many are deceived and unaware that "church work" (not God's work), can lead to sin. There was a time when I was driven and consumed by my work for the church believing that it was connecting me with the right people and building my speaking platform. I was so busy that I started to neglect the needs of my family. In a moment of quiet the Holy Spirit questioned, "Whose work are you doing?" I knew in my heart it wasn't the Lord's.

If you are tired and burned out you are doing your work, not God's. Oftentimes we are working to gain the approval of man, to avoid the quiet that will cause us to reflect on the changes we need to make within ourselves and to feed our egos. (i.e., our sense of importance). Wake up; this is not God's work. It's selfish and leads to destruction.

Stop now and think about your own success or lack thereof. If you are feeling overwhelmed by ministry or other activities pray to God that He reveals His perfect plan for your life. Good success requires that every activity be ordained by God. Remember, not every good endeavor is a God endeavor so seek His will and do as He is instructing (even when it goes against the norm). Godly success is not about making you popular with man but about being right in His sight.

Are you doing it God's way or have you abandoned His plan all together? If the latter, it's never too late to repent and be converted. Today make up your mind to refrain from walking according to the flesh: "For all that *is* in the world—the lust of the flesh, the lust of the eyes, and the pride of life—is not of the Father but is of the world" (1 John 2:16). Endeavor to walk according to the Spirit; He will direct you to succeed God's way.

IS IT GOD'S DESIRE THAT YOU SUCCEED?

First things first; does God want you to succeed? The answer is a resounding yes! In Jeremiah 29:11, the prophet records God's promise to us, "For I know the thoughts that I think toward you, says the LORD, thoughts of peace and not of evil, to give you a future and a hope." With this, God is proclaiming that we have a future, a hope and a call to do great things in Him. You were not born into the wrong family, a mistake, or destined to live a dead end life. God has a plan for you!

The scripture tells us that there is no profit in gaining the world and losing your soul; however, you can gain the world and your soul when you are fully surrendered to God; when you are fully in line with His plans and intentions for your life. I've learned over time that God is a God of abundance and I've come to believe that He has come to give me life and life more abundantly. For that reason, I am not afraid to succeed, knowing that God is with me.

Have you ever considered that you were born for such a time as this; that God has a purpose and a plan for every circumstance in your life and that He has set you up for success? Such was the case for Queen Esther, who was used by God to save her people, the Jews from destruction.

After the dismissal of Queen Vashti, Esther was chosen from many fair maidens, to become King Ahasuerus' wife. How excited she must have been and oh the plans she must have made as she reflected on her good fortune. However, God had other plans. It wasn't His plan that she simply be a trophy wife for King Ahasuerus, but that she would be the vessel God used to save her people from annihilation.

At the time of Esther's reign, Haman, the king's right hand man had an ought with Mordecai, Esther's uncle, which prompted him to plot a scheme against the Jews. He convinced the King to sign a decree that allowed others to kill the Jews at will. Sadly, Esther would not be exempt from annihilation. The words spoken by Mordecai motivated her into action. He stated:

"Do not think in your heart that you will escape in the king's palace any more than all the other Jews. For if you remain completely silent at this time, relief and deliverance will arise for the Jews from another place, but you and your father's house will perish. Yet who knows whether you have come to the kingdom for *such* a time as this?"

Then Esther sent this reply to Mordecai: "Go, gather all the Jews who are present in Shushan, and fast for me; neither eat nor drink for three days, night or day. My maids and I will fast likewise. And so I will go to the king, which *is* against the law; and if I perish, I perish!" (Esther 4:13–16)

And with these words of surrender, she moved into her destiny.

This is the same dedication and passion you need concerning God's plan for your life. You were born for such a time as this—you are not a mistake. There is no one else that can do what you will do or do it how you will do it. Like Queen Esther, be intentional about doing what counts. You should desire to hear the words "well done" not merely from men, but from the One who matters most, your Heavenly Father. He loves you unconditionally and has planned for you to succeed.

PRAYER IS NECESSARY FOR SUCCESS

A tool for ensuring success is prayer. Every surrendered person prays. In fact, the scripture says that we are to pray without ceasing (1 Thessalonians 5:17). Therefore, prayer should be a regular part of your routine and not just what you do first thing in the morning or right before bed. Prayer opens the lines of communication between you and God. It puts you in the posture to hear from Him clearly. Through the active process of prayer, God speaks and reveals His perfect will for your life.

This principle is illustrated in the book of Genesis (I also shared this story in Chapter 5). When Isaac had reached the age of maturity, his father Abraham began the search for his mate. Abraham was determined to find Isaac a wife from his birthplace, Haran. So he charged his chief servant to travel there to find a wife for Isaac amongst his relatives. The servant swore to Abraham that he would succeed. However, this was no small task. The right bride would have to agree to leave all that she knew—her immediate family and friends—to move to a land and family unknown to her. He knew that he needed prayer.

When the servant arrived at his destination he prayed to God the following prayer (Genesis 24:12–14):

> "O LORD God of my master Abraham, please give me success this day, and show kindness to my master Abraham. Behold, *here* I stand by the well of water, and the daughters of the men of the city are coming out to draw water. Now let it be that the young woman to whom I say, 'Please let down your pitcher that I may drink,' and she says, 'Drink, and I will also give your camels a drink'—*let* her *be the one* You have appointed for Your servant Isaac. And by this I will know that You have shown kindness to my master"

Before he had ended his prayer, Rebekah appeared. He immediately asked her for a drink of water. She agreed and also offered to give drink to his camels. He remained silent before God until she was done. Then, knowing that God had granted him success, he bowed his head and worshipped Him. Surrender had truly advanced Abraham's servant.

Pastor John K. Jenkins Sr. has a similar story of how God assisted him with selecting his bride. He placed an engagement ring in the glove compartment of his car, locked it, and prayed that his girlfriend (now his wife) would reach for the glove box and ask why it was locked. Sure enough, as they rode along, she mentioned that she had misplaced her glasses and proceeded to pull on the handle of the glove compartment. She then stated, "Why is this locked?" He immediately pulled over and proposed.

SUCCESS AND FAILURE

Success is the achievement of something desired, planned, or attempted. We often equate success with positive outcomes, but rarely with mere attempts or negative outcomes. However, failure, in the truest sense of the word, is operating outside God's will. All else is perceived failure. When events don't turn out the way we expect we instantly label the venture a failure and feel disappointment. However, from God's vantage point, you are right in line with His successful plan for your life. Therefore, we must put our expectations in God and not our circumstances or feelings. We serve a God that is faithful. His promises to us are sure and will come to pass in their season. If God calls you to do something He will cause you to succeed.

When God called Moses to deliver the children of Israel from Egypt, He did so knowing that Pharaoh would not readily comply with Moses' request. After the first denial some would have given up, but Moses had faith in God's plan. He didn't let rejection or fear stop him from completing God's instructions. He knew that man's "no" would turn into a "yes" if he persisted. And his persistence paid off. He was successful at leading the Israelites out of Egypt. Surrendered advanced Moses despite the obstacles.

In graduate school, I learned of a technique called *reframing,* which is the process of looking at and thinking about beliefs, ideas, or relationships from a different perspective. It's not simply positive thinking; it's the practice of viewing situations from another point of view. Consider the positive effects on your psyche if you would view certain events—being passed up for a promotion, a broken engagement, not getting that appointment as ministry leader—blessings in disguise. Joyce Meyer says that "rejection is God's protection." The thing that you think you need and just can't live without might be the worst thing for you. God knows this and in his sovereignty allows us to lose in the short-term so that we can succeed in the long-term. This is not failure but God's way of making it all right.

However, for some people, the fear of failure is so debilitating that they remain in a state of stagnation. The fear stops all progress; plans lay dormant for years and procrastination becomes their constant companion. Instead of moving forward, they become sidetracked by the details hoping to avoid failure and its associated pain. However, that is not how faith works. God will often call you to do something that doesn't make logical sense because He delights in confounding the logic of man (see 1 Corinthians 1:27). I have made plenty of God-ordained decisions that didn't even make sense to me because I am surrendered. If you know you are doing as God has instructed, don't be thwarted by a roadblock or closed door. God is working it out for your good.

Abraham Lincoln, 16th President of the United States (1861–1865), failed tremendously prior to being elected president. He lost eight elections, failed twice at business, and suffered a nervous breakdown. Yet he dared to believe in himself and sought the highest office of the land and attained it.

At one point in my childhood, my parents were facing foreclosure. God had promised to work it out, and they believed despite the notice that they were to vacate their home. My father didn't fear failure. He went right on praising God for deliverance. God heard him and answered his prayer. On the day we were to be formally evicted, God worked a miracle. The city employee assigned to the case came to our home that day and proceeded to tell my mother that the family would need to evacuate the premises. However, as he spoke he began to look puzzled. My mother inquired and he proceeded to tell her that his records now indicated that the debt had been paid in full. God may not show up when you want, but He is always on time! There is no true failure in God.

CONTENT WITH EACH SUCCESS

On a lunch break at a women's conference, my friend shared her heart. She was deeply troubled by her lack of appreciation for God's blessings on her life. He had allowed her to meet success yet she wasn't satisfied. For her there never seemed an appropriate time to sit back and enjoy the fruit of her labor as she was constantly striving for the next goal. She was growing weary and needed a change

Like my friend, you too may be tired of running the performance treadmill; you are drained and burnout is imminent. Truth be told, the flesh is never satisfied; its cravings are immeasurable. If you live by your flesh you will always strive in vain for the next promotion, degree, job, home, and car. You will always long for what you don't have: a spouse, child, book deal, and television show. Just as God blesses you to be on AM radio, you're clamoring for FM; you're matriculating at a community college but you long to be accepted at a major university. Ecclesiastes 5:10a reads, "He who loves silver will not be satisfied with silver; nor he who loves abundance, with increase." Our fleshly cravings are insatiable and satisfaction eludes the person that is ungrateful and discontent with their present circumstances.

King Solomon, the wisest man to ever live, spoke of the dangers of busyness in Ecclesiastes 2. At the end of his life he felt unfulfilled because he had followed his plan and given in to his every whim. He wrote in verses 17 and 18, "Therefore I hated life because the work that was done under the sun *was* distressing to me, for all *is* vanity and grasping for the wind. Then I hated all my labor in which I had toiled under the sun, because I must leave it to the man who will come after me." His labor would be in vain because he had done all for his own selfish pleasure and gain. He missed this important point. Our fulfillment comes from God, through surrender, obedience and doing what He has called us to do. It is only through surrender that we are advanced.

The scripture reads, "But seek first the kingdom of God and His righteousness, and all these things shall be added to you" (Matthew 6:33).When you seek God and His plan for your life, your striving becomes meaningful and not just a means of getting to the next goal. You must stop achieving for the sake of achieving and start achieving to glorify God. Setting goals is fine but they must be set for the purposes of completing God's work not meeting your fleshly desires.

Paul wrote in Philippians 4:11–13, "Not that I speak in regard to need, for I have learned in whatever state I am, to be content: I know how to be abased, and I know how to abound. Everywhere and in all things I have learned both to be full and to be hungry, both to abound and to suffer need. I can do all things through Christ who strengthens me." This contentment comes from knowing that you are on this Earth to please God and not man. Armed with this belief, you only endeavor to do what God has assigned. Pursue God-opportunities and leave the good opportunities for those who are doing their own will, because it will profit you nothing if you gain the whole world and lose your soul.

My prayer for you is that you surrender your all to God without fear. That you allow His Jeremiah 29:11 plan for you to come to pass in your life. And that you are Surrendered4Life, doing His Will—His Way—All the Time!

Acknowledgements

Without the support and encouragement of my husband, Andel, this book and the other accomplishments would have been much harder to achieve, if they would have been achieved at all. Thank you for all your love and support.

Without my parents, Pastor Donald and Lady Chisholm, who believed in me more than I believed in myself, I'm not sure I would have had enough faith in God to surrender it all.

Much love to my two special gifts, AJ and Aaliyah whom I pray come to love the process of surrender as much as I do.

Special thanks for Pastor John K. and Lady Trina Jenkins whose love and support enables me to live courageously.

To Sundra Ryce, thanks for partnering with me in this calling. Love you like a sister!

To Tiffany Williams, thank you for all you do to make Surrender 365 shine!

To our staff and host of volunteers: Stephanie, Karen, LaToya, Warren, Kim, Josephine, Jessica, Sonya, Bronique, Charmaine, Natalie, I love doing life and ministry with you. Thanks for what you do and who you are!

About the Author

Dr. Celeste Owens is a lover of Jesus, wife to Andel and mom to Andel Jr. and Aaliyah. She travels the world teaching and spreading the philosophy of surrender.

In 2014, she and Andel co-founded Dr. Celeste Owens Ministries, an international healing ministry, whose mission is to equip people to live free and whole through surrender of mind, body, and spirit.

Celeste knows all about surrender and its ability to advance. In 2009, in what she calls an Abraham moment God called her leave all that she knew—private practice, public speaking, and ministry leadership. And in an act of radical obedience she did. From that place of humility and surrender God birthed her first book *The 40-Day Surrender Fast*, a devotional designed to help the reader develop a more intimate relationship with God.

An accomplished scholar, Celeste holds a Bachelor of Arts in Psychology from the State University of New York at Buffalo, a Master of Science in Applied Counseling Psychology from the University of Baltimore and a Doctorate of Philosophy in Counseling Psychology from the University of Pittsburgh.

A breast cancer survivor, Celeste has personally experienced the advancing power of surrender. In 2010 she surrendered her diet to God and through the process of fasting adopted a clean-eating lifestyle. In fact, her personal battle with cancer inspired her to become a Certified Natural Health Professional. Now this once self-proclaimed "junk-food-junkie" is thriving post cancer and inspires others to do the same.

God has provided an opportunity for Celeste to meet the needs of the poor and bring the philosophy of surrender in a very practical way though the non-profit Surrender 365, the mission's arm of Dr. Celeste Owens Ministries. Surrender 365 helps people all over the world to develop a deeper relationship with God and experience the liberating power of surrender to Him through teaching and preaching of God's word. Surrender 365 also facilitates the provision of critically-needed goods and services to the poor and needy.

Surrender is what Celeste does. She will continue to encourage others where ever she may go to do God's Will—His Way—All the Time!

Learn more at: www.drcelesteowens.com

CPSIA information can be obtained
at www.ICGtesting.com
Printed in the USA
LVHW011329081222
734778LV00015B/535

9 780983 789529